TORT LAW

Linda Chadderton

Series editors: Amy Sixsmith and David Sixsmith

First published in 2021 by Fink Publishing Ltd

British Library Cataloguing in Publication Data
A catalogue record for this book is available from the British Library
ISBN: 9781914213069

This book is also available in various ebook formats.
Ebook ISBN: 9781914213137

Multiple-choice questions advisor: Mark Thomas
Cover and text design by BMLD (bmld.uk)
Production by River Editorial
Typeset by Westchester Publishing Services
Commissioning by R Taylor Publishing Services
Development Editing by Peter Hooper
Indexing by Terence Halliday

Fink Publishing Ltd
E-mail: hello@revise4law.co.uk
www.revise4law.co.uk

Contents

About the author

Linda Chadderton is a lecturer in law on the undergraduate LLB and postgraduate Legal Practice Course at UCLAN, and a solicitor and fellow of the Higher Education Academy. As a practising solicitor she specialised in defendant litigation. She teaches tort law, litigation, personal injury, clinical negligence and professional skills. Her experience of working in the legal profession for 20 years and subsequently teaching the next generation of legal professionals means she is ideally placed to understand the issues and application involved in preparing for the SQE.

Series editors

Amy Sixsmith is a senior lecturer in law and programme leader for LLB at the University of Sunderland, and a senior fellow of the Higher Education Academy.

David Sixsmith is a senior lecturer in law and programme leader for LPC at the University of Sunderland, and a senior fellow of the Higher Education Academy.

Introduction to Revise SQE

Welcome to *Revise SQE*, a new series of revision guides designed to help you in your preparation for, and achievement in, the Solicitors Qualifying Examination 1 (SQE1) assessment. SQE1 is designed to assess what the Solicitors Regulation Authority (SRA) refers to as 'functioning legal knowledge' (FLK); this is the legal knowledge and competencies required of a newly qualified solicitor in England and Wales. The SRA has chosen single best answer multiple-choice questions (MCQs) to test this knowledge, and *Revise SQE* is here to help.

PREPARING YOURSELF FOR SQE

The SQE is the new route to qualification for aspiring solicitors, introduced in September 2021 as one of the final stages towards qualification as a solicitor. The SQE consists of two parts:

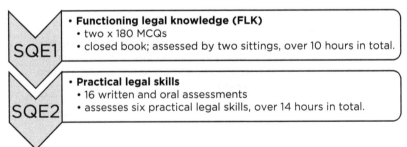

SQE1
- **Functioning legal knowledge (FLK)**
- two x 180 MCQs
- closed book; assessed by two sittings, over 10 hours in total.

SQE2
- **Practical legal skills**
- 16 written and oral assessments
- assesses six practical legal skills, over 14 hours in total.

In addition to the above, any candidate will have to undertake two years' qualifying work experience. More information on the SQE assessments can be found on the SRA website; this revision guide series will focus on FLK and preparation for SQE1.

It is important to note that the SQE can be perceived to be a 'harder' set of assessments than the Legal Practice Course (LPC). The reason for this, explained by the SRA, is that the LPC is designed to prepare candidates for 'day one' of their training contract; the SQE, on the other hand, is designed to prepare candidates for 'day one' of being a newly qualified solicitor. Indeed, the SRA has chosen the SQE1 assessment to be 'closed book' (ie without permitting use of any materials) on the basis that a newly qualified solicitor would know all of the information being tested, without having to refer to books or other sources.

With that in mind, and a different style of assessments in place, it is understandable that many readers may feel nervous or wary of the SQE. This is especially so given that this style of assessment is likely to be different from what readers will have experienced before. In this *Introduction* and revision guide series, we hope to alleviate some of those concerns with guidance on preparing for the SQE assessment, tips on how to approach single best answer MCQs and expertly written guides to aid in your revision.

What does SQE1 entail?

SQE1 consists of two assessments, containing 180 single best answer MCQs each (360 MCQs in total). The table below breaks down what is featured in each of these assessments.

Assessment	Contents of assessment ('functioning legal knowledge')
FLK assessment 1	• Business law and practice • Dispute resolution • Contract • Tort • The legal system (the legal system of England and Wales and sources of law, constitutional and administrative law and European Union law and legal services)
FLK assessment 2	• Property practice • Wills and the administration of estates • Solicitors accounts • Land law • Trusts • Criminal law and practice

Please be aware that in addition to the above, ethics and professional conduct will be examined pervasively across the two assessments (ie it could crop up anywhere).

Each substantive topic is allocated a percentage of the assessment paper (eg 'legal services' will form 12–16% of the FLK1 assessment) and is broken down further into 'core principles'. Candidates are advised to read the SQE1 Assessment Specification in full (available on the SRA website). We have also provided a *Revise SQE checklist* to help you in your preparation and revision for SQE1 (see below).

HOW DO I PREPARE FOR SQE1?

Given the vastly different nature of SQE1 compared to anything you may have done previously, it can be quite daunting to consider how you could possibly prepare for 360 single best answer MCQs, spanning 11 different substantive topics (especially given that it is 'closed book'). The *Revise SQE FAQs* below, however, will set you off on the right path to success.

Revise SQE FAQs

Question	Answer
1. Where do I start?	We would advise that you begin by reviewing the assessment specification for SQE1. You need to identify what subject matter can be assessed under each substantive topic. For each topic, you should honestly ask yourself whether you would be prepared to answer an MCQ on that topic in SQE1.
	We have helped you in this process by providing a *Revise SQE checklist* on our website (revise4law.co.uk) that allows you to read the subject matter of each topic and identify where you consider your knowledge to be at any given time. We have also helpfully cross-referenced each topic to a chapter and page of our *Revise SQE* revision guides.
2. Do I need to know legal authorities, such as case law?	In the majority of circumstances, candidates are not required to know or use legal authorities. This includes statutory provisions, case law or procedural rules. Of course, candidates will need to be aware of legal principles deriving from common law and statute.
	There may be occasions, however, where the assessment specification does identify a legal authority (such as *Rylands v Fletcher* in tort law). In this case, candidates will be required to know the name of that case, the principles of that case and how to apply that case to the facts of an MCQ. These circumstances are clearly highlighted in the assessment specification and candidates are advised to ensure they engage with those legal authorities in full.

Revise SQE FAQs (continued)

Question	Answer
3. Do I need to know the history behind a certain area of law?	While understanding the history and development of a certain area of law is beneficial, there is no requirement for you to know or prepare for any questions relating to the development of the law (eg in criminal law, candidates will not need to be aware of the development from objective to subjective recklessness). SQE1 will be testing a candidate's knowledge of the law as stated at the date of the assessment.
4. Do I need to be aware of academic opinion or proposed reforms to the law?	Candidates preparing for SQE1 do not need to focus on critical evaluation of the law, or proposed reforms to the law either.
5. How do I prepare for single best answer MCQs?	See our separate *Revise SQE* guide on preparing for single best answer MCQs below.

Where does *Revise SQE* come into it?

The *Revise SQE* series of revision guides is designed to aid your revision and consolidate your understanding; the series is not designed to replace your substantive learning of the SQE1 topics. We hope that this series will provide clarity as to assessment focus, useful tips for sitting SQE1 and act as a general revision aid.

There are also materials on our website to help you prepare and revise for the SQE1, such as a *Revise SQE* checklist. This *checklist* is designed to help you identify which substantive topics you feel confident about heading into the exam – see below for an example.

Revise SQE checklist

Tort Law

SQE content	Corresponding chapter	*Revise SQE checklist*		
		I do not know this subject and I am not ready for SQE1 ☐	I partially know this subject, but I am not ready for SQE1 ☐	I know this subject and I am ready for SQE1 ☐

Tort Law (continued)

SQE content	Corresponding chapter	Revise SQE checklist		
Negligence (duty of care)	Chapter 1	I do not know this subject and I am not ready for SQE1 ☐	I partially know this subject, but I am not ready for SQE1 ☐	I know this subject and I am ready for SQE1 ☐
Negligence (breach)	Chapter 1	I do not know this subject and I am not ready for SQE1 ☐	I partially know this subject, but I am not ready for SQE1 ☐	I know this subject and I am ready for SQE1 ☐

PREPARING FOR SINGLE BEST ANSWER MCQS

As discussed above, SQE1 will be a challenging assessment for all candidates. This is partly due to the quantity of information a candidate must be aware of in two separate sittings. In addition, however, an extra complexity is added due to the nature of the assessment itself: MCQs.

The SRA has identified that MCQs are the most appropriate way to test a candidate's knowledge and understanding of fundamental legal principles. While this may be the case, it is likely that many candidates have little, if any, experience of MCQs as part of their previous study. Even if a candidate does have experience of MCQs, SQE1 will feature a special form of MCQs known as 'single best answer' questions.

What are single best answer MCQs and what do they look like?
Single best answer MCQs are a specialised form of question, used extensively in other fields such as in training medical professionals. The idea behind single best answer MCQs is that the multitude of options available to a candidate may each bear merit, sharing commonalities and correct statements of law or principle, but only one option is absolutely correct (in the sense that it is the 'best' answer). In this regard, single best answer MCQs are different from traditional MCQs. A traditional MCQ will feature answers that are implausible in the sense that the distractors are

'obviously wrong'. Indeed, distractors in a traditional MCQ are often very dissimilar, resulting in a candidate being able to spot answers that are clearly wrong with greater ease.

In a well-constructed single best answer MCQ, on the other hand, each option should look equally attractive given their similarities and subtle differences. The skill of the candidate will be identifying which, out of the options provided, is the single best answer. This requires a much greater level of engagement with the question than a traditional MCQ would require; candidates must take the time to read the questions carefully in the exam.

For SQE1, single best answer MCQs will be structured as follows:

A woman is charged with battery, having thrown a rock towards another person intending to scare them. The rock hits the person in the head, causing no injury. The woman claims that she never intended that the rock hit the person, but the prosecution allege that the woman was reckless as to whether the rock would hit the other person.

The factual scenario. First, the candidate will be provided with a factual scenario that sets the scene for the question to be asked.

Which of the following is the most accurate statement regarding the test for recklessness in relation to a battery?

A. There must have been a risk that force would be applied by the rock, and that the reasonable person would have foreseen that risk and unjustifiably taken it.

B. There must have been a risk that force would be applied by the rock, and that the woman should have foreseen that risk and unjustifiably taken it.

C. There must have been a risk that force would be applied by the rock, and that the woman must have foreseen that risk and unjustifiably taken it.

D. There must have been a risk that force would be applied by the rock, and that both the woman and the reasonable person should have foreseen that risk and unjustifiably taken it.

E. There must have been a risk that force would be applied by the rock, but there is no requirement that the risk be foreseen.

The question. Next, the candidate will be provided with the question (known as the 'stem') that they must find the single best answer to.

The possible answers. Finally, the candidate will be provided with **five** possible answers. There is only one single best answer that must be chosen. The other answers, known as 'distractors', are not the 'best' answer available.

Now that you know what the MCQs will look like on SQE1, let us talk about how you may go about tackling an MCQ.

How do I tackle single best answer MCQs?

No exact art exists in terms of answering single best answer MCQs; your success depends on your subject knowledge and understanding of how that subject knowledge can be applied. Despite this, there are tips and tricks that may be helpful for you to consider when confronted with a single best answer MCQ.

1. Read the question twice	2. Understand the question being asked	3. If you know the answer outright	4. If not, employ a process of elimination	5. Take an educated and reasoned guess	6. Skip and come back to it later

1. Read the entire question at least twice

This sounds obvious but is so often overlooked. You are advised to read the entire question once, taking in all relevant pieces of information, understanding what the question is asking you and being aware of the options available. Once you have done that, read the entire question again and this time pay careful attention to the wording that is used.

- **In the factual scenario:** Does it use any words that stand out? Do any words used have legal bearing? What are you told, and what are you not told?
- **In the stem:** What are you being asked? Are there certain words to look out for (eg 'should', 'must', 'will', 'shall')?
- **In the answers:** What are the differences between each option? Are they substantial differences or subtle differences? Do any differences turn on a word or a phrase?

You should be prepared to give each question at least two viewings to mitigate any misunderstandings or oversights.

2. Understand the question being asked

It is important first that you understand what the question is asking of you. The SRA has identified that the FLK assessments may consist of single best answer MCQs that, for example,

- require the candidate to simply identify a correct legal principle or rule
- require the candidate to not only identify the correct legal principle or rule, but also apply that principle or rule to the factual scenario
- provide the candidate with the correct legal principle or rule, but require the candidate to identify how it should be properly applied and/or the outcome of that proper application.

By first identifying what the question is seeking you to do, you can then understand what the creators of that question are seeking to test and how to approach the answers available.

3. If you know the answer outright

You may feel as though a particular answer 'jumps out' at you, and that you are certain it is correct. It is very likely that the answer is correct. While you should be confident in your answers, do not allow your confidence (and perhaps overconfidence) to rush you into making a decision. Review all of your options one final time before you move on to the next question.

4. If you do not know the answer outright, employ a process of elimination

There may be situations in which the answer is not obvious from the outset. This may be due to the close similarities between different answers. Remember, it is the 'single best answer' that you are looking for. If you keep this in your mind, it will thereafter be easier to employ a process of elimination. Identify which answers you are sure are not correct (or not the 'best') and whittle down your options. Once you have only two options remaining, carefully scrutinise the wording used in both answers and look back to the question being asked. Identify what you consider to the be the best answer, in light of that question. Review your answer and move on to the next question.

5. Take an educated and reasoned guess

There may be circumstances, quite commonly, in which you do not know the answer to the question. In this circumstance, you should try as hard as possible to eliminate any distractors that you are positive are incorrect and then take an educated and reasoned guess based on the options available.

6. Skip and come back to it later

If time permits, you may think it appropriate to skip a question that you are unsure of and return to it before the end of the assessment. If you do so, we would advise

- that you make a note of what question you have skipped (for ease of navigation later on) and
- ensure you leave sufficient time for you to go back to that question before the end of the assessment.

The same advice is applicable to any question that you have answered but for which you remain unsure.

We hope that this brief guide will assist you in your preparation towards, and engagement with, single best answer MCQs.

GUIDED TOUR

Each chapter contains a number of features to help you revise, apply and test your knowledge.

Make sure you know   Each chapter begins with an overview of the main topics covered and why you need to understand them for the purpose of the SQE1 assessments.

SQE assessment advice   This identifies what you need to pay particular attention to in your revision as you work through the chapter.

What do you know already?   These questions help you to assess which topics you feel confident with and which topics you may need to spend more time on (and where to find them in the chapter).

Key term   Key terms are highlighted in bold where they first appear and defined in a separate box.

Exam warning   This feature offers advice on where it is possible to go wrong in the assessments.

Revision tip   Throughout the chapters are ideas to help you revise effectively and be best prepared for the assessment.

Summary   This handy box brings together key information in an easy to revise and remember form.

Practice example   These examples take a similar format to SQE-type questions and provide an opportunity to see how content might be applied to a scenario.

Procedural link   Where relevant, this element shows how a concept might apply to another procedural topic in the series.

Key point checklist   At the end of each chapter there is a bullet-point summary of its most important content.

Key terms and concepts   These are listed at the end of each chapter to help ensure you know, or can revise, terms and concepts you will need to be familiar with for the assessments.

0

0

SQE-style questions Five SQE-style questions on the chapter topic give you an opportunity to test your knowledge.

Answers to questions Check how you did with answers to both the quick knowledge test from the start of the chapter and the SQE questions at the end of the chapter.

Key cases, rules, statutes and instruments These list the key sources candidates need to be familiar with for the SQE assessment.

SQE1 TABLE OF LEGAL AUTHORITIES

The SQE1 Assessment Specification states the following in respect of legal authorities and their relevance to SQE1:

> On occasion in legal practice a case name or statutory provision, for example, is the term normally used to describe a legal principle or an area of law, or a rule or procedural step (eg *Rylands v Fletcher*, CPR Part 36, Section 25 notice). In such circumstances, candidates are required to know and be able to use such case names, statutory provisions etc. In all other circumstances candidates are not required to recall specific case names, or cite statutory or regulatory authorities.

This *SQE1 table of legal authorities* identifies the legal authorities you are required to know for the purpose of the SQE1 Functioning Legal Knowledge assessments for *Tort Law.*

Legal authority	Corresponding *Revise SQE* chapter/pages
Occupiers' Liability Act 1957	Chapter 6, pages 115–121
Occupiers' Liability Act 1984	Chapter 6, pages 121–124
Consumer Protection Act 1987	Chapter 7, pages 140–143
Rylands v Fletcher *[1868] LR 3 HL 330 (HL)*	Chapter 8, pages 166–169

TABLE OF CASES

TABLE OF STATUTES

1

Negligence: Duty of care and breach

■ MAKE SURE YOU KNOW

This chapter will cover two of the four main elements of negligence – duty of care and breach of duty. You are required to know the elements of negligence and apply the legal principles and rules appropriately and effectively to realistic client-based ethical problems and situations for your SQE1 assessment. The figure below highlights the four elements which need to be present to successfully bring a claim in negligence.

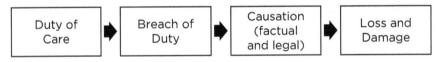

Duty of Care ➡ Breach of Duty ➡ Causation (factual and legal) ➡ Loss and Damage

Elements of negligence

■ SQE ASSESSMENT ADVICE

As you work through this chapter, remember to pay particular attention in your revision to:
• the steps required in establishing negligence
• situations where there is an established duty of care
• situations where there is no established duty of care
• what breach of duty entails and the standard of care applied.

■ WHAT DO YOU KNOW ALREADY?

Have a go at these questions before reading this chapter. If you find some difficult or cannot remember the answers, make a note to look more closely at that during your revision

1) What are the necessary elements to successfully bring a claim in negligence?
    [Introduction to negligence, page 2]

2) In which of the following examples is there an established duty of care?

   a) doctor and patient
   b) driver and pedestrian
   c) teacher and pupil
   d) solicitor and client

   [Establishing a duty of care, pages 5-8]

3) What are the two approaches the courts use when they are considering whether a duty of care is owed?

   [Establishing a duty of care, pages 5-8]

4) What test do the courts use in establishing the general standard of care?

   [Standard of care, pages 15-18]

5) What are the special situations where the court applies a different standard of care?

   [Standard of care: special situations, pages 18-20]

INTRODUCTION TO NEGLIGENCE

The everyday use of the word **negligence** conjures up the notion of a failure to take proper care of something. The law recognises this concept and seeks to provide a remedy to those that are caused injury by a wrongdoer failing to take proper care. The tort of negligence concentrates on the link between the wrongdoer's act or omission and whether that risk ought to have been foreseen.

Negligence is a large topic and will be covered in three chapters. This first chapter will deal with duty and breach. The second chapter will deal with causation, remoteness and loss. The third chapter will deal with remedies, claims for economic loss and psychiatric injury.

Key term: negligence

Negligence relates to an act or omission which breaches a duty of care owed by one party (defendant) to another (claimant) and as a consequence causes loss and damage to that party (claimant).

Revision tip

The SQE1 Assessment Specification does not require you to know case names but it will assist with your understanding and revision if you know the case name and the legal principle.

DUTY OF CARE

When looking at negligence as part of your SQE revision, the first element you need to prove in establishing a claim in negligence is to show that there was a legal **duty of care** owed by the defendant to the claimant. **Figure 1.1** shows the steps involved in establishing liability in negligence.

Was the claimant owed a duty of care?

Has the defendant breached that duty by falling below the required standard of care?

Was the defendant's breach of duty the factual cause of the claimant's injury?

Was the damage suffered not too remote?

Figure 1.1: Duty of care

There are established categories of relationships where a duty of care exists and there are situations where the common law has developed duties of care. **Table 1.1** highlights some examples of situations where a duty of care has been established.

Table 1.1: Examples of established duty of care situations

Duty owed by:	Duty owed to:
Doctor	Patient
Dentist	Patient
Road user (motorists, cyclists etc)	Road user (pedestrians, motorists, cyclists etc)
Teacher	Pupil
Lecturer	Student
Employer	Employee
Manufacturer	Consumer

Key term: duty of care

Duty of care relates to the obligation owed by the defendant to the claimant to take care to avoid causing the claimant injury or loss.

Look at **Practice example 1.1** below and think about whether a duty of care exists here.

> ## Practice example 1.1
>
> You and your friend decide to meet for a drink in a café. You order and pay for both drinks. The café owner brings you the drinks. Your friend's drink is in an opaque bottle and the café owner pours half of the drink into your friend's glass. As she finishes the glass, she pours the residue of the bottle into her glass. It is then she sees what appears to be the remains of a snail and realises she has ingested whatever was in the bottle already. She becomes ill with gastroenteritis.
>
> Do you think the café owner or the manufacturer of the drink owes your friend a duty to take care, namely a duty not to allow the bottled drink to become contaminated and make her ill?
>
> These were the facts in *Donoghue v Stevenson* [1932] AC 562 (HL). Mrs Donoghue could not bring a claim in contract against the café owner as she had no contract with him as her friend paid for the drink. She brought an action against Stevenson, the manufacturer of the ginger beer drink. The House of Lords had to decide whether a duty of care existed. Did the manufacturer owe a duty to ensure the drink did not contain elements that would make the ultimate consumer ill? The House of Lords found that the manufacturer owed a duty to ensure that the drink did not contain material which would make the consumer of the drink ill. Donoghue was able to successfully seek damages for her injuries.

Donoghue v Stephenson established the **neighbour principle**. Lord Atkin stated that:

> You must take reasonable care to avoid acts or omissions which you can reasonably foresee would be likely to injure your neighbour. Who, then, in law is my neighbour? The answer seems to be persons who are so closely and directly affected by my act that I ought reasonably to have them in contemplation as being so affected when I am directing my mind to the acts or omissions which are called in question.

Each case which comes before the courts turns on its own facts, meaning that the court will look at the facts and decide whether as a starting point there is a duty of care.

Establishing a duty of care

In 1990 the courts developed a legal principle for establishing whether a duty of care exists following the case of *Caparo Industries plc v Dickman* [1990] 2 AC 605 (HL). The case involved investors (Caparo) relying upon accounts prepared by auditors (Dickman) relating to Fidelity plc. Once Caparo had bought shares in Fidelity they realised that Fidelity's accounts were in a poor state, which caused Caparo to incur financial losses. The Court had to decide whether Dickman owed a duty of care to Caparo.

The House of Lords stated that courts should use two approaches when considering whether there was a duty of care owed:

a) incrementally and by analogy, or

b) a three-stage test.

Incrementally and by analogy

This first approach taken by the courts means that if a duty of care has been found to exist previously, looking to precedents decided by the courts, or where the situation is analogous to one in which a duty of care has been found to exist, the court will use that to decide the case without any need to refer to the *Caparo* three-stage test.

Caparo three-stage test

The second approach to establishing a duty of care means you must establish the following:

- Reasonable foresight that the defendant's failure to take care could cause damage to the claimant; and
- That there was a relationship of proximity (ie, some connection) between the claimant and the defendant; and
- It is fair, just and reasonable that the law should recognise a duty on the defendant to take reasonable care not to cause that damage to the claimant.

Table 1.2 gives an overview of the *Caparo* three-stage test and highlights examples of how the courts have considered the test. In considering whether there is a duty of care, these examples will help you to understand how the test can be applied.

The *Caparo* three-stage test will only be used in a small number of cases where the court will have to decide whether a new category of duty of care exists. It is not a prescriptive test but it allows the courts to consider whether it is fair to impose a duty of care.

Table 1.2: Overview of Caparo three-stage test

Legal principle	Examples of cases to demonstrate the principle
Reasonable foreseeability The claimant must fall within a class of individuals put at foreseeable risk by the defendant's action	Children playing in the loading bay of the defendant's premises and developing mesothelioma in adult life. It was reasonably foreseeable that the plaintiffs would be exposed to the risk of lung damage. *Evelyn Margereson v JW Roberts Ltd* [1996] 4 WLUK 21 A pregnant pedestrian suffering shock and stillbirth following the sight of the aftermath of a cycling accident. It was not reasonably foreseeable that all people on the street where the negligent driver drove would suffer injury. *Bourhill v Young* [1943] AC 92
Proximity Before a duty of care can arise, there needs to be a certain type of relationship or connection between the parties	A boxer collapsed during the final round of a fight. Resuscitation equipment was not available at the ring side and as a result he suffered brain damage. The Board, as the only body in the UK which could license professional boxing matches and control what medical assistance was available at the ringside, had a relationship of sufficient proximity. Boxers should be able to rely on the defendant to look after their safety. *Watson v British Boxing Board* [2001] 2 WLR 1256 A surveyor employed by a landlord of shop premises (Maison Blanc) failed to notify the owners who were renting the shop that the sign above the shop was defective. When the sign fell and injured the claimant the surveyors were not liable. There was insufficient proximity between the surveyor and Maison Blanc (shop proprietor), or between the surveyor and the general public, to establish a duty of care. *Harrison v Technical Sign Co Ltd and Active Commercial Interiors v Cluttons* [2013] EWCA Civ 1569

Overview of Caparo three-stage test (continued)

Legal principle	Examples of cases to demonstrate the principle
Fair, just and reasonable Policy considerations are taken into account to prevent a 'flood' of claims	A claim for compensation for wrongful birth following a negligently performed sterilisation operation on the father failed. Whilst it is fair and reasonable to impose a duty of care on the doctor performing the operation it was unfair to extend it to the costs of raising the child (pure economic loss). The pleasure of raising a child outweighed the financial burden. *McFarlane v Tayside Health Board* [2000] 2 AC 59 It was fair, just and reasonable to impose a duty of care on a rugby referee in an amateur adult match to minimise dangers to players as players' safety was dependent upon the rules of the game being enforced. *Vowles v Evans* [2003] 1 WLR 1607

Figure 1.2 explains the steps the court can consider when dealing with new cases and establishing whether a duty of care exists.

Is there an existing precedent?	
Yes – follow that precedent	No – proceed to next step

Is there an analogous precedent similar to the case you are considering?	
Yes – that precedent can be extended to either establish or deny a duty of care	No – proceed to next step

Is there reasonable foreseeability of harm? (*Caparo* three-stage test)	
Yes – go to next step	No – no duty of care owed

Is there a relationship of proximity between the claimant and defendant? (*Caparo* three-stage test)	
Yes – go to next step	No – no duty of care owed

Is it fair, just and reasonable to impose a duty of care? (*Caparo* three-stage test)	
Yes – duty of care owed	No – no duty of care owed

Figure 1.2: Establishing a duty of care – new cases

Revision tip

Remember that if you are presented with a series of facts where there is an established duty of care you will not need to consider the three-stage test.

Special duty of care problems (omissions and third parties)

In considering whether there is a duty of care, there will be occasions when the harm has been caused due to:
- a party failing to act (omissions) or
- where the incident has been caused by a third party.

The courts have developed these 'special duty' problem areas by modifying the *Caparo* test in certain situations. What follows is a consideration of these special areas.

Omissions

In the law of negligence there is no positive duty to act outside tortious or contractual relationships between parties. This means that there is no duty owed in respect of omissions (failing to act) and the law does not impose liability. If you walk past a person choking on food and do not stop and perform first aid you will not be held liable in negligence. There is no positive duty to stop and perform first aid. **Practice example 1.2** considers omissions and failure to positively act.

Practice example 1.2

A local authority is aware of a dangerous obstruction at a junction. It has discretionary statutory power (Highways Act 1980 s 79) to have the obstruction removed and there have been three previous accidents at the same junction. The local authority fails to remove the obstruction and a further serious accident occurs.

Would the local authority be liable for their failure/omission to positively act and remove the obstruction?

These were the facts in *Stovin v Wise* [1996] AC 923 (HL). The Court found that a statutory power did not give rise to a common law duty of care and the local authority had not acted unreasonably in failing to proceed under that power. Even if the work ought to have been carried out, it could not be found that a public law

duty gave rise to an obligation to compensate those suffering loss due to its non-performance. The creation of a duty of care in the circumstances posed an unacceptable risk to local authority budgetary decision making in an area where road users themselves were subject to compulsory insurance requirements.

Remember that the law does impose obligations for omissions where there is an established relationship. These 'relationships' are the exceptions to the rule that there is no positive duty to act to prevent harm. **Table 1.3** shows some examples where a duty of care is imposed for omissions due to an established relationship.

Table 1.3: Examples of liability for omissions

Relationship	Case example
Control Situations where the defendant exercises control over the claimant and as such a duty of care for omissions should be imposed.	A teacher who had allowed a child to run onto the road (causing the death of a lorry driver when he swerved and hit a telegraph pole in trying to avoid the child) in the process of attending to another pupil owed the same duty of care as a careful parent. The teacher was not to blame for the accident, but the school (Council) was liable for their omission – in not having a precaution to prevent the child getting onto the street. *Carmarthenshire County Council v Lewis* [1955] AC 549 (HL)
Assumptions of responsibility Situations where the defendant has assumed responsibility for the claimant's safety/wellbeing.	A naval pilot celebrating his birthday became so drunk he collapsed and the officer in charge ordered he be put to bed. He later died due to choking on his own vomit. The Court found that the duty was not owed to prevent the deceased from drinking too much. The duty was however owed for a different omission, namely, the officer on duty's failure to have someone stationed to watch him whilst he slept. *Barrett v Ministry of Defence* [1995] 1 WLR 1217 (CA)

Examples of liability for omissions (continued)

Relationship	Case example
Creating/adopting risks Where the defendant creates a dangerous situation there will be a positive duty to act to deal with the danger.	A tree was stuck by lightning and caught fire (in Western Australia). The owner of the land had a tree-feller cut the tree down but omitted to extinguish the fire and allowed it to burn out. The fire spread to neighbouring land. The landowner was negligent in omitting to extinguish the fire with water. In omitting to take any further steps to prevent the fire from spreading he had adopted the risk of it spreading and was liable when it did. *Goldman v Hargrave* [1967] 1 AC 645 (PC)

Third parties

There is no general duty of care in relation to the acts of third parties. The law does not recognise a duty to prevent other people from causing harm. However, there are exceptions to this rule, similar to the exceptions discussed in respect of omissions. The exceptions originate from a relationship between the parties. **Practice example 1.3** highlights one of these exceptions.

Practice example 1.3

A supermarket chain purchases a cinema with a view to demolishing it and building a supermarket. A few weeks after purchase a fire breaks out, thought to be started by the act of a third party – intruders. The fire destroys the cinema and adjoining properties. Is the supermarket chain liable to the owners of the adjoining properties? Did the supermarket owners owe a duty of care to the property owners to ensure that the cinema was kept locked, preventing vandals from breaking in and starting a fire?

These were the facts in *Smith v Littlewoods; Maloco v Littlewoods* [1987] AC 241 (HL) 271. The supermarket owners had no knowledge

of any previous attempts and as such the court found that it was not reasonably foreseeable by them that the fire would be started nor that it would engulf the building.

In *Smith* Lord Goff stated that a duty of care could arise in four circumstances:
- where there was a special relationship between the claimant and defendant
- where there is a special relationship between the defendant and a third party, such as a relationship of control or supervision
- where someone creates a source of danger and it is reasonably foreseeable that the third party would interfere
- where there is a failure to take steps to stop the danger created by a third party.

Table 1.4 gives examples of cases where liability for third parties was established by the court.

Table 1.4: Examples of liability for third parties

Exceptions	Examples
Special relationship between claimant and defendant A relationship such that there is 'proximity' between the parties.	Defendant (decorator) and claimant (homeowner). Duty on defendant to lock premises when he left. *Stansbie v Troman* [1948] 2 KB 48 (CA)
Special relationship between defendant and third party The more 'proximate' the relationship between the parties the more likely there will be a duty of care imposed.	Supervisors of young offenders (who escaped and caused damage to boats) owed a duty of care to owners of the boats. *Home Office v Dorset Yacht Co Ltd* [1970] AC 1004 (HL)
Creation of a source of danger A duty of care may be imposed on the defendant where the third party's actions make the situation worse.	Defendant owed a duty of care to a police officer who was injured in the process of trying to control the defendant's untethered horses after they bolted due to children (third party) throwing stones. *Haynes v Harwood* [1935] 1 KB 146 (CA)

Examples of liability for third parties (continued)

Exceptions	Examples
Failure to prevent a known danger A duty of care may be imposed where the third party creates the danger (as opposed to where the defendant creates the danger).	Defendant (local authority) liable to owners of adjoining premises in failing to prevent the spread of fire by third party intruders. The local authority knew of the danger and failed to prevent it. *Clark Fixing Ltd v Dudley Metropolitan Borough Council* [2001] EWCA Civ 1898

Revision tip

Remember that if you are presented with a series of facts relating to an act or an omission in one of these special categories the duty of care will be modified.

The courts have also considered whether there should be liability for criminal acts of third parties. For example, the courts have decided that the owner of a hotel with adequate security would not owe an absolute duty to prevent an attack on one of the hotel guests (*Al-Najar and others v The Cumberland Hotel (London) Ltd* [2019] 1 WLR 5953).

Consider **Practice example 1.4.**

Practice example 1.4

Following neighbour disputes in local authority housing, a resident repeatedly behaving in an anti-social manner is advised by the local authority that they have commenced eviction proceedings against him. The resident then returns home and attacks and kills the person whom he believes to be the cause of the complaint.

Did the local authority have a duty of care to warn or protect the deceased from the criminal acts of a third party?

These were the facts in the case of *Mitchell v Glasgow City Council* [2009] UKHL 11. The court applied the test of fairness and public policy (*Caparo*) and held that it was not just, fair and reasonable that the local authority should be held liable. The court set out examples where there would be a duty to warn another person that he was at risk of loss, injury or damage as a result of the criminal act of a third party:

- where the person was under a duty to supervise the acts of the third party and fails to do so (*Dorset Yacht*)
- where a person specifically creates a risk of injury (eg, if he arms someone with a weapon)
- where a person assumes specific responsibility for the claimant's safety and then carelessly fails to protect him
- where an employer is vicariously liable for his employee's crime (see **Chapter 5**).

Summary: duty of care	
WHAT is duty of care?	A duty of care is the obligation owed by the defendant to the claimant to avoid causing the claimant loss or damage.
WHEN is duty of care established?	There are situations where an established duty of care exists. For example, the duty of care owed by road users to other road users, by doctors to patients, and by teachers to pupils. For new cases consider whether there is an existing precedent and follow that. If not, if there is an analogous precedent follow that. If not, use the three-stage *Caparo* test (foreseeability of harm, proximity between the parties and whether it is fair, just and reasonable to impose a duty of care).
HOW does it relate to negligence?	Once a duty of care is established the first element of a potential claim in negligence has been proved. This is the first hurdle to cross in bringing a claim in negligence. Once a duty of care has been established, the second hurdle to establish is whether the duty of care has been breached – covered in the next section.

BREACH OF DUTY

When considering scenarios relating to negligence in the SQE assessment, you will need to consider whether a duty of care is established. Once this is established the next element to prove is that the duty of care was breached. There will be a **breach of duty** when the defendant falls below the particular standard of care required by the law. The burden for proving a breach of duty is on the claimant. The court has to be satisfied 'on balance of probabilities' that the duty of care has been breached. We can understand this by using percentage terms. If the court finds that it is 50% likely the claimant's case occurred as the claimant states then the court will find for the defendant. However, if the court finds that it is 51% likely the claimant's case occurred as the claimant states then they will find for the claimant. Whether a breach of duty has occurred depends upon the particular facts of the case. Each case turns on its own facts. **Figure 1.3** can be used to help you establish whether there has been a breach of duty.

Key term: breach of duty
Breach of duty is where one party's behaviour has fallen below the standard expected and required by the law.

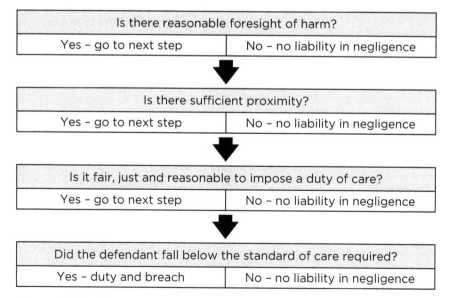

Figure 1.3: Establishing breach of duty

Standard of care

You need to be aware of the different standards of care used by the courts. They are as follows:

• general standard of care
• professional standard of care
• special standard of care.

Standard of care: general

The courts use an objective test to measure what the defendant has done compared to what a 'reasonable man' would have done. If the defendant's actions reflect those actions of a reasonable person then they will not have breached their duty of care. If the defendant's actions do not reflect those of a reasonable person they will have breached their duty of care. Their actions will have fallen below the **standard of care**.

Key term: standard of care

The standard of care relates to tests the court will use to assess whether the defendant's actions are those of a reasonable person, in all the circumstances.

There are significant cases where the court has tried to define the reasonable person. **Table 1.5** identifies these cases. Remember that the SQE1 Assessment Specification will not require you to recall the names of the cases but it is important that you understand the principles.

Table 1.5: Reasonable person – case law

Who is the reasonable person?	Examples – case law
'Negligence is the omission to do something which a reasonable man, guided upon those considerations which ordinarily regulate the conduct of human affairs, would do, or doing something which a prudent and reasonable man would not do.' (Lord Alderson)	The defendant's water main burst, flooding the claimant's house. The defendant had acted in accordance with the average temperatures in previous years, not the severe unexpected temperature of 1855. A reasonable man would have done no different. *Blyth v Proprietors of the Birmingham Waterworks* (1856) 11 Ex Ch 781

Reasonable person – case law (continued)

Who is the reasonable person?	Examples – case law
'Some persons are by nature unduly timorous and imagine every path beset by lions. Others, of more robust temperament, fail to foresee or nonchalantly disregard even the most obvious dangers. The reasonable man is presumed to be free both from over-appreciation and from over-confidence.' (Lord Macmillan)	The defendant was not liable when an employee spilt hot tea on the child claimant whilst carrying an urn. The defendant had assumed the urn would be carried carefully. The reasonable man would not be so apprehensive of danger. *Glasgow Corporation v Muir* [1943] AC 448 (HL)
'The man on the Clapham Omnibus.' 'The man who in the evening pushes his lawn mower in his shirtsleeves.' (Lord Greer)	The defendants were not liable to race track spectators killed in an accident the reasonable person could not foresee. *Hall v Brooklands Auto-Racing Club* [1933] 1 KB 205 (CA)
'... commuters on the Underground.' (Lord Steyn)	The reasonable person would not agree that a doctor/hospital should compensate the parents for the cost of bringing up a healthy but unwanted child, following negligent sterilisation surgery. *McFarlane v Tayside Health Board* [2000] 2 AC 59

In conclusion, for the SQE1, when considering scenarios relating to negligence, you need to be aware that the reasonable person is the 'average person', and in considering the standard of care, it is this average objective test the courts use.

Standard of care: professional

The courts recognise a different standard of care in respect of certain categories of defendants.

Defendants purporting to possess a skill or profession will be judged by a reasonable person with that same skill or trained in the same profession. Consider **Practice example 1.5**.

Practice example 1.5

A hospital patient undergoes electroconvulsive therapy in an attempt to treat severe depression. The treatment involves passing an electric current through the patient's head, which causes seizures. During treatment the patient sustains double hip and pelvis fractures.

Is the doctor negligent in failing to provide the claimant with muscle relaxants or restraints which may have prevented the injuries? Should the doctor have warned the patient about the risks associated with the treatment?

These were the facts in *Bolam v Friern Hospital Management Committee* [1957] 1 WLR 582 (QBD). The court had to decide whether the reasonable doctor would have administered relaxants, restrained the claimant and warned the claimant about the risks of the treatment. The court accepted that there was a responsible body of experts opposed to the use of relaxant drugs and restraint. Further that the experts would only have warned the claimant had he enquired about the risks (which were small) of the treatment.

The *Bolam* test established that a doctor would not be deemed to have breached their duty of care if they acted in accordance with a competent body of medical opinion. In these cases, expert evidence from others within the profession is used to determine whether the defendant's actions were reasonable in the circumstances. The *Bolam* test was modified in *Bolitho v City and Hackney Health Authority* [1998] AC 232 (HL). In *Bolitho* the claimant suffered brain damage as a result of the failure of a doctor to attend to the claimant and intubate (place a tube down the patient's throat to assist with breathing). The court accepted that there were differing medical opinions as to whether the claimant should have been intubated. The court had to satisfy itself that the 'responsible body of medical men' could state a logical basis for the opinion they supported (not intubating the claimant).

When dealing with these types of scenarios in the SQE1 assessment, remember that when presented with skilled medical professionals the standard of care is as follows:
• Did the doctor act in a manner accepted by a responsible body of medical professionals?
• If so, is there a logical basis for their acting in such a manner?

Bolam and *Bolitho* deal with treatment. There has been a departure from the *Bolam* test in respect of the disclosure of pre-treatment information, which you should also ensure you understand. **Practice example 1.6** illustrates further development of the legal principle relating to warning patients of material risks.

Practice example 1.6

For insulin-dependent diabetic pregnant women there is a 9–10% risk of shoulder dystocia during birth. A diabetic pregnant woman of small stature is not advised of this risk and during the birth of her baby there are complications which lead to oxygen deprivation and the child being born with cerebral palsy. The doctor chose not to advise his patient of the risks as he knew them to be small and that most women would opt for a caesarean had he done so. Had his patient known the risks she would have opted for a caesarean. Is the doctor negligent in not advising the patient about the risks?

These were the facts in *Montgomery v Lanarkshire Health Board* [2015] UKSC 11. The Court held that a duty of care extended to warning patients about material risks. The court established that rather than being a matter of clinical judgement it was a matter for the patient to make a decision in respect of their treatment knowing the material risks involved. Whether a risk is a material risk is determined by whether a reasonable person in the patient's position would be likely to attach significance to the risk. In other words, the doctor should disclose risks that they know or ought to know the patient would view as significant.

The court does not recognise that junior professionals may have less experience than their senior colleagues. It is no defence to a claim to cite lack of experience. This was established in the case of *Wilsher v Essex Area Health Authority* [1988] AC 1074.

Standard of care: special situations
There are certain situations where the courts apply a different standard of care. **Table 1.6** highlights these special situations.

Table 1.6: Standard of care: special situations

Special standard of care	Examples – case law
Children Children are judged by the standard of those of a similar age.	Two 15-year-old schoolgirls were fencing with plastic rulers during class when one of the rulers snapped and a fragment of plastic caused damage to the claimant's sight. The defendant was not liable as an ordinary 15-year-old would not have foreseen the risk. *Mullin v Richards* [1998] 1 WLR 1304 (CA)
Sporting activities Duty only where there is a reckless disregard for safety.	An experienced horse rider injured a photographer at a horse show when he lost control of his horse. There was no breach of duty as there was no 'reckless disregard' for the safety of the spectator, only an error of judgement by the defendant. *Wooldridge v Summer* [1963] 2 QB 43 (CA)
Unskilled defendant Judged to a reasonably competent standard.	A learner driver collided with a lamp post, injuring her driving instructor. The defendant was liable as she was judged to the standard of a reasonably competent driver, not the learner driver she was. *Nettleship v Weston* [1971] 2 QB 691
Illness On occasion modified, the standard of care of a reasonably competent (driver).	The defendant suffered a stroke as his journey began but carried on driving and had three collisions. He was liable as he should have stopped the moment he felt ill. *Roberts v Ramsbottom* [1980] 1 WLR 823 The defendant driver suffered low blood sugar, causing lack of glucose to the brain, and crashed his lorry. He was not liable as he had no knowledge or warning of his condition. *Mansfield v Weetabix* [1998] 1 WLR 1263

Standard of care: special situations (continued)

Special standard of care	Examples – case law
Emergency situations The duty is to exercise such care and skill as was reasonable in all the circumstances.	The fire service had to transport equipment in order to respond to an emergency. They did not have the means to secure the equipment and the claimant fire fighter was injured when he had to travel with it in the back of the truck. The defendant was not liable – there was not a breach of duty as the benefit of saving a life outweighed the need to take precautions. *Watt v Hertfordshire County Council* [1954] 1 WLR 835 (CA) A police officer who injured the suspect he was pursuing at high speed owed the same standard of care to the suspect as to everyone else. *Marshall v Osmand* [1983] 3 WLR 13
State of knowledge Judged at the time of the incident.	Patients suffered paralysis following contaminated anaesthetic injections. At the time it was not known that the vials storing the anaesthetic could develop cracks allowing bacteria to form. The court judged the case by the state of knowledge at the time (1947) of the incident. *Roe v Minister of Health* [1954] 2 QB 66 (CA)

Revision tip

The SQE1 Assessment Specification expects you to understand the general standard of care and the professional standard of care. Ensure you understand the difference between everyday situations (eg, road traffic accidents) and those involving professionals or people with a particular set of skills (eg, doctors, dentists, solicitors etc). **Table 1.1** highlights examples of established duty of care situations.

Other relevant factors when considering the standard of care

Before we move on to the next element of negligence which must be proved in order to successfully make a claim, it is important to be aware that the court also takes into consideration other relevant factors when considering the standard of care. Other relevant factors are:
- cost of precautions
- social value
- likelihood of harm
- seriousness of injury.

Table 1.7 covers these other relevant factors with case examples to explain what the court takes into consideration.

Table 1.7: Standard of care – other relevant factors

Other relevant factors relating to the standard of care	Case example
Cost of precautions: If the defendant could have avoided breaching their duty of care by taking low-cost precautions the court is more likely to find that the defendant fell below the standard expected and breached their duty to the claimant.	Owners of a factory that had sustained flooding after severe rainstorms had done all that was reasonable (spreading sawdust on the floor) to prevent employees slipping. It was unreasonable to send the employees home as it would mean shutting the factory, which would be very costly. *Latimer v AEC Ltd* [1952] 2 QB 701 (CA)
Social value: The courts may apply a lower standard of care where the defendant's behaviour is in society's interest.	Playing a game in the dark added no social value, only excitement, and the Scout Association were liable for the scout's injuries sustained when playing the game. *Scout Association v Barnes* [2010] EWCA Civ 1486

Standard of care – other relevant factors (continued)

Other relevant factors relating to the standard of care	Case example
	The Compensation Act 2006 allows the court to take into consideration whether the steps the defendant may have taken relating to a socially desirable activity would have discouraged those from taking part or prevented them from doing so. It reinforces the common law by reassuring people that they should not be deterred from taking part in risky activities if they are for the greater good.
	Also, the Social Action, Responsibility and Heroism Act 2015 (SARAH) complements the Compensation Act and seeks to provide protection for those that seek to help in emergency situations. When considering the breach of duty, the court is required to have regard to whether the person was acting for the benefit of society, whether they demonstrated a responsible approach and whether they were acting heroically by intervening in an emergency to assist an individual in danger.
Likelihood of harm: The court will take into account the probability of the injury occurring. The more likely it is that the injury will occur, the more likely the court will find the defendants liable on the basis that they could have avoided it.	Whilst it was probable that a cricket ball could clear the perimeter fence from the cricket ground, the likelihood of it hitting a pedestrian (which it did) was a precaution an ordinary careful man would not take. *Bolton v Stone* [1951] 1 All ER 1078 (HL)
Seriousness of injury: The more serious the injury the more likelihood that the court will find that the defendant has fallen below the required standard of care.	The employer of a garage hand who was blind in one eye should have taken into account the seriousness of the consequences for the claimant of injuring his healthy eye by providing safety goggles. *Paris v Stepney Borough Council* [1951] AC 367 (HL)

You should now understand the main principles of the standard of care and how to address it in your revision. **Figure 1.4** illustrates the elements to be considered when revising standard of care.

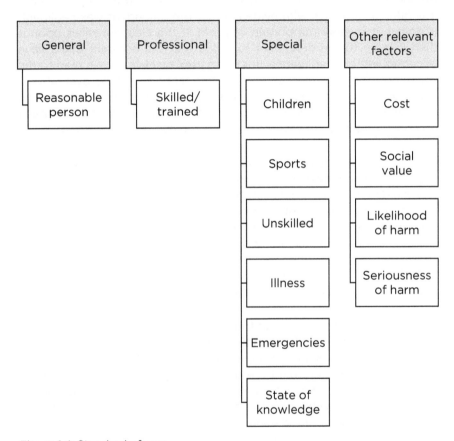

Figure 1.4: Standard of care

ESTABLISHING BREACH OF DUTY

When deciding cases before them, the courts will look at the facts and the evidence and conclude whether the defendant owed a duty of care, whether the duty was breached and whether the breach was both the factual and legal cause of the damage and loss. We will look at causation (factual and legal) in the following chapter.

Res ipsa loquitor

It is important to be aware of the concept of res ipsa loquitur, which is a Latin term meaning 'the thing speaks for itself'. Res ipsa loquitur can be used by the claimant in cases where the actual occurrence of the incident is evidence of negligence. This helps the claimant where it is difficult to prove with evidence that the defendant was negligent. It does not reverse the burden of proof. If the claimant relies upon it then it is up to the defendant to argue that the accident could have occurred without negligence. It is often used by claimants in road traffic accidents. The equivalent of arguing 'the fact you ran me over whilst I was crossing, using a pedestrian crossing, is evidence by itself that you were driving negligently'. In that example if the defendant had not been driving negligently, they would not have run over the pedestrian.

In order to rely on res ipsa loquitur there must be the following present:
• Control – whatever caused the damage must be under the control of the defendant or those that the defendant is responsible for; for example, the operator of heavy machinery which injures employees.
• The damage would not normally occur without negligence; for example, a plane would not normally crash without negligence (whether that be pilot or mechanical error).
• The cause of the accident must be unknown; for example, if a vehicle loses control and passengers in the vehicle are injured.

Remember that if the cause of the accident is known the court will not allow the claimant to rely upon the principle of res ipsa loquitur. In the example of a car losing control, if there are no witnesses, evidence or explanation for the accident the principle may apply. If, however, road conditions were icy and witnesses state they saw the car's brake lights engage and then witnessed the car skid, it is clear that the accident has been caused by the defendant's failure to drive in an appropriate manner for the road conditions.

Civil Evidence Act 1968

Under the Civil Evidence Act 1968 criminal convictions can be used in evidence in civil proceedings (s 11) if the offence the defendant is convicted of involves negligent conduct. This can assist a claimant as a conviction in a criminal court will be taken as proof by the civil court that the defendant did commit the offence. The burden of proof will shift to the defendant to prove that they were not negligent. The most common examples are driving offences. If a defendant motorist who collides with a pedestrian is convicted under s3 of the Road Traffic Act 1988 for driving without due care and attention, it will be up to the defendant to prove that their negligence did not cause the accident. Similarly, if a doctor is convicted of the criminal offence of gross negligence manslaughter due to their grossly negligent medical treatment which exposed their patient to risk of death, it would be up to the defendant to prove that the claimant's death was not caused by their negligence.

Summary: breach of duty	
WHAT is breach of duty?	If the defendant owes the claimant a duty of care and the defendant's behaviour has fallen below the standard expected and required by the law, they will have breached their duty of care owed to the claimant.
WHAT is the standard expected by the law?	The standard of care relates to the test the court will use to assess whether the defendant's actions are those of a reasonable person, in all the circumstances. a) General standard of care – judged by the actions of a reasonable person. b) Professional standard – judged by a reasonable person with that same skill/ trained in the same profession. c) Special situations – modified to take into account the different standard expected.
WHO is the reasonable person?	The reasonable person is the average person, neither too cautious nor too brave.

■ KEY POINT CHECKLIST

This chapter has covered the following key knowledge points. You can use these to structure your revision around, making sure to recall the key details for each point, as covered in this chapter.

- Negligence is a tort which seeks to provide a remedy where loss or damage is caused to an injured party by a wrongdoer's acts or omissions.
- In order to establish a claim in negligence one must first establish that the defendant owed a duty of care to the claimant.

- The courts recognise situations where there is an established duty of care. Where there is no established duty of care the court may use previous precedents for similar circumstances or analogous circumstances. If there are no relevant precedents the court may use the *Caparo* three-stage test.
- The standard of care relates to the test the court will use to decide whether the defendant's actions were those of a reasonable person. If the defendant's acts or omissions fall below the standard of care expected the court will find that the defendant breached their duty of care.
- The courts recognise a different standard of care in respect of certain categories of defendants.
- The courts use an objective test to measure what the defendant has done compared to what a 'reasonable person' would have done. If the defendant's actions reflect those actions of a reasonable person then they will not have breached their duty of care. If the defendant's actions do not reflect those of a reasonable person they will have breached their duty of care. Their actions will have fallen below the standard of care.
- Defendants purporting to possess a skill or profession will be judged by a reasonable person with that same skill or trained in the same profession.
- In deciding whether the defendant breached their duty of care the court will also take into consideration other relevant factors such as cost of precautions, social value, likelihood of harm and seriousness of injury.
- The burden of proof is on the claimant to prove that on balance of probabilities the defendant breached their duty of care owed to the claimant.
- The claimant can be assisted by the doctrine of res ipsa loquitur if the cause of the damage/loss is unknown, would not normally have occurred without negligence and the defendant had sufficient control.
- Where a defendant has been convicted of a criminal offence which involves negligent conduct the claimant can seek to rely upon the conviction and the defendant will need to prove that they were not negligent.

■ KEY TERMS AND CONCEPTS
- negligence (**page 2**)
- duty of care (**page 3**)
- breach of duty (**page 14**)
- standard of care (**page 15**)

■ SQE1-STYLE QUESTIONS

QUESTION 1

A man drives his vehicle along a dual carriageway intending to take the first exit at the roundabout leading off the dual carriageway. When he gets to the roundabout there is a queue of stationary traffic. The traffic moves off slowly and he follows the car in front. Checking the roundabout, he sees it is clear and accelerates onto it. The car in front has stopped as the traffic has slowed down and is now stationary and as a result the man drives his vehicle into a collision with the rear of this vehicle.

Is the man likely to be in breach of his duty of care?

A. No, the car in front should have moved onto the roundabout.

B. Yes, but only if it can be proved that it is fair and reasonable.

C. No, whilst the man owes a duty of care, he has not breached his duty as there is no proximity between the parties.

D. Yes, road users owe other road users an established duty of care and by failing to concentrate and colliding with the vehicle in front the man has breached that duty.

E. No, the collision was not reasonably foreseeable and as such there is no breach of duty.

QUESTION 2

A group of children (aged 13 years) are playing on skateboards at a skate park. One group of children (skaters) are taking it in turns to skate down the ramps at the park whilst another group of children (runners) run in front of them. The aim of the game is for the 'runners' to get from one side of the park to the other without the 'skaters' having to stop or swerve out of the way. One of the runners collides with a skater, causing the skater to fall and fracture his left leg and right arm.

In assessing the negligence of the child that caused the injury, which of the following is the most accurate statement of what the court will consider?

A. Whether a reasonable person would have foreseen the likelihood of harm.

B. Whether a reasonable prudent adult would have realised that there was risk of injury.

C. Whether a reasonable 13-year-old would have realised that there was risk of injury.

D. Whether a reasonable prudent child would have realised that there was risk of injury.

E. Whether the risk of injury was such that a child, irrespective of their age, would have foreseen the likelihood of harm.

QUESTION 3

The fire service is responding to an emergency call. The employee of the fire service driving the fire engine is travelling at 50mph in a 30mph zone. The fire engine is displaying sirens and lights to alert other road users of its presence. The fire engine is travelling on a long straight carriageway at the end of which is a traffic light-controlled junction. The lights are on red for the approaching fire engine. As the road appears clear the driver of the fire engine does not slow down but continues through the red light. Suddenly a vehicle enters the junction from the right and collides with the fire engine.

Which of the following is the most accurate statement as to what the court will take into consideration in determining the standard of care owed by the fire service's employee?

A. The social value of responding to an emergency.

B. The experience of the fire service's employee.

C. The cost of taking precautions.

D. The seriousness of the claimant's injuries.

E. The liability of the other driver.

QUESTION 4

A patient attends the accident and emergency department of the local hospital complaining of symptoms of a blood clot in his lungs. The treating doctor (newly qualified and in his first week at the hospital) examines the patient but does not identify that he has suffered a blood clot in his lungs. The doctor fails to administer medication which would treat the condition and, as a consequence, the patient dies.

In considering whether the treating consultant was negligent, which of the following is the most accurate statement of what the court will consider?

A. Whether the patient gave the requisite consent for the treatment.

B. Whether a majority of medical professionals would have identified the patient's condition.
C. Whether a responsible body of medical experts would have identified the patient's condition.
D. Whether a responsible body of newly qualified doctors would have identified the patient's condition.
E. Whether a majority of newly qualified doctors would have identified the patient's condition.

QUESTION 5

The court is dealing with a claim brought in negligence. When considering whether the claimant owed a duty of care to the defendant it is accepted that there are no analogous or similar precedents in respect of the circumstances involved.

Which of the following is the most accurate statement as to what the court will take into consideration in deciding whether there is a duty of care owed by the defendant to the claimant?

A. Whether it is fair, just and reasonable.
B. Whether the parties have proximity.
C. Whether damage was foreseeable.
D. Foreseeability, proximity and whether it is fair, just and reasonable.
E. Whether failure to take care caused damage.

■ ANSWERS TO QUESTIONS

Answers to 'What do you know already?' questions at the start of the chapter

1) The necessary elements required to bring a successful negligence claim are (i) duty of care, (ii) breach of duty, (iii) causation (factual and legal) and (iv) loss and damage.
2) There is an established duty of care in all of the examples. Doctors must do their patients no harm. Road users must abide by the Highway Code. Teachers are said to be 'in loco parentis' (meaning instead of a parent). Solicitors are professionals regulated by their governing body and must act in the best interests of their clients.

3) The two approaches the court takes into account when considering whether there is a duty of care owed is the *Caparo* three-stage test or incrementally and by analogy.

4) The courts use the reasonable person test when assessing the defendant's (general) standard of care.

5) The situations where the court applies a different standard of care are children; sporting activities; unskilled defendants; illness; emergencies and state of knowledge.

Answers to end-of-chapter SQE1-style questions

Question 1:

The correct answer was D. This is because there is an established duty of care between road users. By failing to keep a safe distance and not concentrating on the vehicle in front the court will likely find that the driver has breached his duty of care. Watch out for situations where there is an established duty of care. There is no need to consider the *Caparo* three-stage test.

A is wrong because the traffic was queueing and it was not possible for the car to proceed.

B is wrong because there is an established duty of care between road users and whether it is fair and reasonable relates to a situation where there may not already be an established duty of care.

C is wrong because as there is an established duty of care between the parties there is no need to consider proximity.

E is wrong because there is an established duty of care and foreseeability in respect of that duty of care is not relevant.

Question 2:

The correct answer was C. This is because the court would consider the standard of care expected by a child of similar age, ie. 13 years old. This is one of the categories where there is a special standard of care.

A is wrong because the court will take into consideration the child's age and not that of a 'reasonable person'.

B is wrong because the child is not a reasonably prudent adult.

D is wrong because the court will always take into consideration the child's age.

E is wrong because the court will consider the standard of care expected by a 13-year-old child.

Question 3:

The correct answer was A. This is because there is social value in attending to an emergency. Even though the court will take this into consideration, they are unlikely to conclude that the fire service's driver was reasonable in failing to slow down at the traffic light-controlled junction. The benefit of getting to the emergency quicker does not outweigh the risk of causing the collision. So, whilst the court will consider the social value, they may still find the defendant liable.

B is wrong because the standard of care (road user driving an emergency vehicle) is not affected by the experience of the claimant.

C is wrong because cost of taking precautions is not relevant to the issues.

D is wrong because seriousness of injuries is not taken into consideration when deciding whether the claimant owed a duty of care.

E is wrong because the question asks about the duty of care owed by the fire service's employee not the fault of the other driver.

Question 4:

The correct answer was C. This is because the court considers whether a responsible body of medical experts would have identified the patient's condition. If so, the doctor will have fallen below the standard of care and be in breach of his duty of care. Watch out for the level of experience. Remember that the court will judge a junior doctor to the same standard of care as a fully qualified senior doctor if that is what the role at the hospital purports to be.

A is wrong as, irrespective of whether the patient consented to any treatment, the doctor fell below the standard of care expected.

B is wrong because the test does not refer to a 'majority' of medical professionals.

D is wrong because the court will not take into account the doctor's lack of experience.

E is wrong because the court will consider whether a responsible body of medical experts would have ascertained the claimant was suffering with a blood clot.

Question 5:

The correct answer was D. This is because if there is no analogous precedent or similar case the court uses a three-stage test – the court will consider whether there was reasonable foresight that the defendant's failure to take care could cause damage to the claimant; and whether there was a relationship of proximity between the claimant and the defendant; and whether it is fair, just and reasonable that the law should recognise a duty on the defendant to take reasonable care not to cause damage to the claimant.

A, B and C are wrong because they are only individual elements of the three-stage test.

E is wrong because the court will consider whether to impose a duty of care before then going on to consider whether the breach/ failure to take care caused the damage.

■ KEY CASES, RULES, STATUTES AND INSTRUMENTS

The SQE1 Assessment Specification does not require you to know case names, but it is helpful to know the names of the cases for memory recall purposes.

* *Donoghue v Stevenson* [1932] AC 562 (HL) (*neighbour principle*)
* *Caparo Industries plc v Dickman* [1990] 2 AC 605 (HL) (*Caparo three-stage test*)
* *Bolitho v City and Hackney Health Authority* [1998] AC 232 (HL)
* *Bolam v Friern Hospital Management Committee* [1957] 1 WLR 582 (QBD) (*Bolam test*)
* *Montgomery v Lanarkshire Health Board* [2015] UKSC 11

2

Negligence:
Causation, remoteness and loss

■ MAKE SURE YOU KNOW

The previous chapter concentrated on the first two elements to be proved in establishing negligence (duty of care and breach of duty). This chapter concentrates on the two remaining elements required to prove negligence, namely causation and loss. You are required to know the elements of negligence and apply the legal principles and rules appropriately and effectively to realistic client-based ethical problems and situations for your SQE1 assessment.

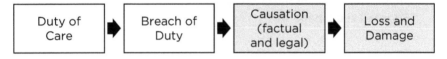

Elements of negligence

■ SQE ASSESSMENT ADVICE

As you work through this chapter, remember to pay particular attention in your revision to:
• steps required in proving factual causation
• situations where there are multiple possible causes of damage
• situations where there are multiple sufficient causes of damage
• steps required in proving legal causation
• the consequence of a break in the chain of causation.

■ WHAT DO YOU KNOW ALREADY?

Have a go at these questions before reading this chapter. If you find some difficult or cannot remember the answers, make a note to look more closely at that during your revision.
1) What is the 'but for' test?
   [Factual causation, pages 35–44]

2) What are the exceptions to the 'but for' test?

   [Factual causation, pages 35–44]

3) True or false?

   Legal causation relates to whether the negligent act was the legal cause of the claimant's harm and if the loss/damage is too remote the claimant will not be liable.

   [Legal causation, pages 44–48]

4) What is a novus actus interveniens?

   a) an omission which displaces the claimant's responsibility but which the claimant remains liable for

   b) an act which creates further damage, which the claimant remains liable for

   c) an act which breaks the chain of causation, making the claim likely to succeed

   d) an act which breaks the chain of causation, allowing the defendant to escape liability

   [Intervening acts, pages 46–48]

5) What is the eggshell skull principle?

   [Eggshell skull, page 46]

INTRODUCTION TO CAUSATION, REMOTENESS AND LOSS

Once you have established that the defendant breached their duty of care to the claimant the next requirement is to establish that the breach caused the claimant's harm. For the purpose of the SQE1 assessment you are required to understand:

• causation

• remoteness and loss.

Each of these will be dealt with throughout the chapter. To begin with, however, it's worth noting that **causation** has two distinct parts: the first is factual causation and the second is legal causation. The court will look at whether the breach of duty was the cause in fact of the harm (factual causation) and whether on the legal interpretation of the facts the harm was not too remote (legal causation). **Figure 2.1** highlights what the court will take into consideration when dealing with causation.

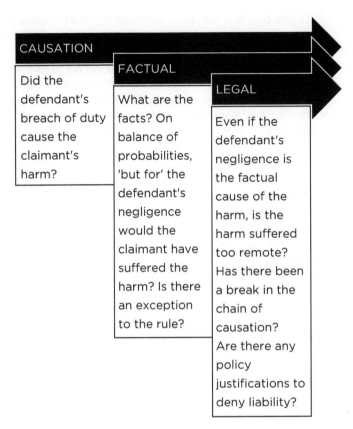

Figure 2.1: Factual and legal causation

Key term: causation

Causation relates to the connection between the breach of duty and the harm suffered. The breach of duty must be both the factual and legal cause of the harm.

FACTUAL CAUSATION

The connection between the breach of duty and the harm suffered needs to be proved by the claimant. The claimant must prove that the defendant's actions caused 'in fact' the claimant's harm. To determine this, the courts use the 'but for' test. The 'but for' test means that the court will look at the defendant's breach of duty and ask, 'But for the defendant's breach of duty would the harm have occurred?' If the answer is 'no', the harm would not have occurred but for the defendant's negligence then the court will find that the defendant's negligence is the factual cause of the claimant's harm. The 'but for' test is explained in *Barnett v Chelsea and Kensington Hospital Management Committee* [1969] 1 QB 428 (QBD). In *Barnett* a doctor did not physically examine the claimant when he attended the hospital's casualty department and the claimant later died from arsenic poisoning. The doctor admitted negligence (he owed a duty of care and had breached that duty) but denied he had caused the claimant's death because even if the doctor had acted he could not have saved the claimant as it was too late to do so. The court held that the failure to treat the claimant was not the cause of death. The claimant was destined to die due to the fact he had ingested arsenic. Therefore the harm would have occurred in any event and not 'but for' the doctor's negligence.

Problems proving factual causation

For *single cause* harm situations, the 'but for' test will be used by the court. However, there are situations with complex facts where it is not possible to establish liability using the 'but for' test because there may be many potential causes of harm. In these complex cases the courts have established exceptions to the test. The exceptions are:
• multiple potential causes
• multiple sufficient causes
• lost chance.

Figure 2.2 illustrates the issues involved in proving factual causation.

Multiple potential causes

In cases where there are competing causes of harm, the percentage chance of one of the causes being the sole cause of the harm reduces. To prepare for the SQE assessment, when dealing with competing cause cases, consider whether there is enough evidence to prove that the harm has been caused by the defendant's negligence. There may be an innocent cause competing with a guilty cause of harm. The breach of duty may also not be the sole cause but may have materially contributed to the harm or materially increased the risk of

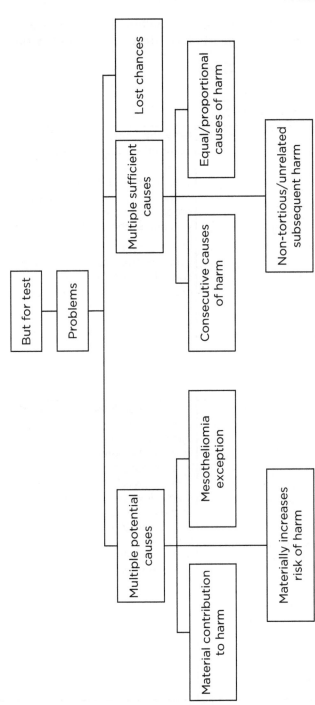

Figure 2.2: Factual causation – problems with the 'but for' test

harm. **Table 2.1** illustrates the type of multiple potential causes and highlights cases where the courts have developed case law dealing with these issues.

Table 2.1: Multiple potential causes

Example case	How the court dealt with the competing causes of harm
Competing causes: *Wilsher v Essex Area Health Authority* [1988] AC 1074 (HL) A doctor negligently fails to monitor the oxygen in the blood of a baby born prematurely and twice gives the baby too much oxygen. Too much oxygen in the blood is a known cause of a retinal condition which causes blindness, which the baby developed. However, there were also four other possible causes of the condition.	Each *competing cause* had a 20% chance of being the factual cause of the condition. On balance of probabilities the doctor's negligence was one of the five factual causes. The court found that on the evidence the cause of the baby's condition could not conclusively be proved to be down to the doctor's negligence.
Materially contributed to harm: *Bonnington Castings Ltd v Wardlaw* [1956] AC 613 A factory worker contracts a lung condition (pneumoconiosis) from the inhalation of silica dust. Inhalation of the dust was inevitable due to the nature of his job. Some of the dust was inhaled due to the nature of the job (innocent dust), whilst some of the dust was inhaled due to the fact that the employer had not ventilated the factory properly (guilty dust). Is the employer liable where it cannot be established which dust has caused the condition?	The lung condition is a cumulative disease caused by the build-up of silica dust in the lungs. On balance, 'but for' the defendant's negligence it could not be proved that the claimant would have suffered the harm. However, the combination of the guilty dust and the innocent dust were more likely to cause the disease. The court found the employer liable as their negligence had *materially contributed* to the harm.

Multiple potential causes (continued)

Example case	How the court dealt with the competing causes of harm
Materially increases the risk of harm: *McGhee v National Coal Board* [1973] 1 WLR 1 (HL) The claimant worked cleaning the defendant's brick kilns. He was exposed each day to brick dust during his work. There were no washing facilities at the defendant's premises and the claimant would cycle home covered in grime and sweat. The claimant contracted dermatitis, which can be triggered by one exposure to dust. Is the employer liable when it is not possible to distinguish which dust caused the condition?	With similar facts to *Bonnington* (but with the exception that dermatitis is not cumulative), the court had to decide whether the innocent exposure to dust during the day caused the condition or the guilty exposure when he cycled home and it remained on his skin. The court found the employers negligent on the basis that the longer the dust was on someone's skin the *greater the risk* of developing dermatitis. This increased risk was enough to establish causation.

The court further developed the multiple potential cause exception to the 'but for' test in the case of *Fairchild v Glenhaven Funeral Services Ltd* [2003] 1 AC 32 (HL). The claimants developed lung cancer (mesothelioma) which can be caused by a single fibre of asbestos. They had worked for several employers during their careers and could not show on balance of probabilities which employer had exposed them to the fatal fibre. The court applied *McGhee* as the employers had materially increased the risk of harm. The court found the employers jointly and severally liable, meaning each employer was liable for the whole loss and each also liable for their share of the loss.

Figure 2.3 is an example of the Fairchild exception which will help you understand the position should you encounter an SQE1 question which involves a mesothelioma claim. The claimant has five different periods of employment (including self-employment). Company 1 and 2 went into insolvency so the claimant will not be able to recover any damages from them. Using the decision in *Fairchild* the court will find that company 3 and 4 are both jointly and severally liable. This means that the claimant can pursue a claim against either company 3 or 4 and receive 100% of the damages from either one; equally he can pursue a claim against both company 3 and 4 and he will still receive 100% of the damages. (In practice company 3 and 4 will probably agree to contribute equally to the claim.)

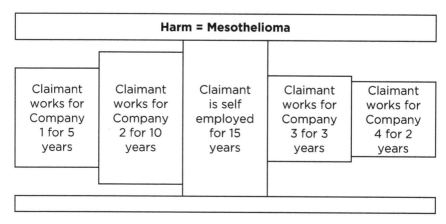

Figure 2.3: Fairchild exception example

Fairchild was considered in *Barker v Corus UK Ltd* [2006] 2 AC 572 (HL). In *Barker* the claimant had been exposed to asbestos over three periods during his career. The first period was working for a company (now insolvent), the second working for the defendant and the third whilst working for himself. The court (applying *Fairchild*) found the defendant and the insolvent company jointly and severally liable but reduced the claimant's damages by 20% to reflect the period when the claimant was self-employed. As one of the employers was insolvent the claimant wanted the other defendant to bear the additional proportion of the damages. The court disagreed and found that the negligent defendants should only be responsible (proportionately) for the extent to which they had increased the risk for the claimant.

Compensation Act 2006

Parliament reacted to the decision in *Barker* by passing the Compensation Act 2006 which effectively saw the position revert back to *Fairchild*. Section 3 provides that a claimant suffering from mesothelioma can recover damages from all responsible persons in breach – the responsible person being both jointly and severally liable.

Revision tip

Ensure you understand the position regarding mesothelioma claims is the *Fairchild* position reiterated in the Compensation Act 2006, namely that each employer can be pursued, and the employers will be jointly and severally liable.

Fairchild relates to mesothelioma cases where there have been multiple negligent exposures to asbestos. **Practice example 2.1**, in contrast, deals with an example of where there was only one negligent exposure.

Practice example 2.1

A claimant (deceased) worked in the defendant's factory offices in Ellesmere Port for 20 years. She was exposed to areas within the factory that were contaminated by asbestos, but she was also exposed to low levels of asbestos in the general environment around her local area. Is the factory owner liable proportionately for the 20-year exposure (*Barker*)? Or liable for the whole loss (*Fairchild*)?

In *Sienkiewicz v Greif Ltd* [2001] UKSC 10, the court decided that the *Fairchild* exception also applied to claims where there was only one negligent defendant. The defendant had materially increased the risk of the claimant developing the disease and as such was 100% liable.

Mesothelioma Act 2014
Due to difficulties involved in tracing employers, parliament passed the Mesothelioma Act 2014 which allows claimants who contracted the disease after 2012 to claim compensation from a government fund.

The *Fairchild* exception also applies to claimants who have developed lung cancer due to exposure to asbestos. As the Compensation Act 2006 only applies to mesothelioma, if a claimant develops lung cancer due to asbestos exposure he could successfully claim against any or all of the employers subjecting him to negligent exposure, but the damages would be apportioned as per *Barker*.

Exam warning

In dealing with SQE questions about employer's claims involving exposure to asbestos ensure you consider the claimant's illness. If the claimant suffers from mesothelioma the Compensation Act 2006 (joint and several liability) is the position. If the claimant develops lung cancer due to negligent exposure to asbestos then *Barker* is the position, namely that the claimant can claim from any liable employers, but the damages will be apportioned relating to how long the claimant worked for that employer.

Multiple sufficient causes

Where more than one negligent defendant could have caused the harm, the court will find both defendants liable. Difficulties can arise where one defendant's negligent act occurs after an earlier negligent act of a previous defendant. Both defendants pass the 'but for' test, but which one should be liable for the harm? **Practice example 2.2** is an example case.

Practice example 2.2

The claimant pedestrian's leg is severely injured due to the negligent driving of the defendant. The claimant is unable to continue with his current employment and takes a job in a scrapyard. During an armed robbery at the scrapyard his same leg is shot and subsequently has to be amputated. The defendant (driver) argued that their liability ended as the claimant was no longer suffering pain due to the leg being removed.

The court found that the liability for the original accident continued even after the claimant had been shot in _Baker v Willoughby_ [1970] AC 467 (HL). The second injury to the leg could not reduce the defendant driver's liability or the amount of damages due to the claimant.

In _Jobling v Associated Dairies Ltd_ [1982] AC 794 (HL) the court had to consider a similar situation as _Baker_. The claimant suffered a back injury during the course of his employment but was then diagnosed with a back disease unrelated to the injury. The court had to consider whether the defendant should be responsible for the continuing claim (greater loss of earnings due to back disease) and held that the compensation should cease at the point the defendant was diagnosed with back disease, as this would have happened in any event.

Revision tip

When dealing with questions involving consecutive causes of harm, all passing the 'but for' test, the original defendant will be responsible for the harm. If there is an unrelated or non-tortious cause of subsequent harm which does not pass the 'but for' test the original defendant will not be liable for that subsequent harm.

The above cases deal with claims where it is possible to prove which defendant caused the harm. The court has also considered cases where it is impossible to prove which defendant is liable. **Practice example 2.3** considers an example of this.

Practice example 2.3

A pedestrian crosses a road and is hit by the first negligent motorist and then immediately by a second negligent motorist. It is impossible to establish which motorist has caused the claimant's injuries. Using the 'but for' test results in both defendants being 50–50 responsible and neither satisfying liability on balance of probabilities. Which, if any, of the defendants are liable?

This is what the court had to consider in *Fitzgerald v Lane* [1989] AC 328 (HL). The court applied *McGhee* and using the material increase in risk of harm concluded that both defendants were equally liable.

Table 2.2 gives a summary of the relevant principles used in determining causation.

Table 2.2: Determining factual causation

Single cause of harm	The 'but for' test
Competing cause of harm	The breach that substantially causes the harm will be sufficient to prove causation
Materially contributed to harm	The breach that materially contributed to the harm will be sufficient to prove causation
Materially increases the risk of harm	The breach that materially increases the risk of harm will be sufficient to prove causation

Lost chance

We have considered competing causes of harm (whether consecutive – one after the other, or concurrent – at the same time) but what about a negligent act that increases the risk of something happening? **Practice example 2.4** illustrates how the court deals with these types of 'lost chance' claims.

Practice example 2.4

A young boy falls out of a tree and attends hospital with an injured hip. The doctors fail to diagnose vascular necrosis. He returns five days later and receives the correct diagnosis; however, they are unable to prevent paralysis. Had he received the correct diagnosis initially there would have been a 25% chance of the condition being prevented. The claimant had a 75% chance of developing the condition in any event. Did the loss of this 25% chance of recovery satisfy the civil burden on balance of probabilities?

This is what the court had to consider in *Hotson v East Berkshire Health Authority* [1987] AC 750 (HL). The claimant failed as the court applied the 'but for' test and found that it could not be said on balance that but for the doctor's negligence the claimant would have avoided the condition. There was a 75% chance he would have developed the condition even if treated immediately and correctly.

Exam warning

When considering SQE1 questions about loss of chance remember that if the 'lost chance' is less than 50% then on balance of probabilities the court is unlikely to find for the claimant. If the question relates solely to clinical negligence, then you need to be aware that a lost chance claim cannot form the basis of the claim.

LEGAL CAUSATION

The final element in establishing negligence is to prove legal causation. Having proved that the breach of duty was the factual cause of the claimant's harm the court will consider whether the breach of duty was the real cause in law of the claimant's harm. In doing this the court will consider whether the harm suffered was too remote a consequence of the breach and whether there have been any intervening acts which could break the chain of causation.

REMOTENESS

The **test of remoteness** involves asking whether the harm suffered was too remote a consequence of the defendant's negligence. The courts have considered whether liability can be limited for the consequences of a negligent act. **Practice example 2.5** considers this issue.

Key term: test of remoteness

Was the type/kind of damage reasonably foreseeable at the time that the breach of duty occurred?

Practice example 2.5

Owners of a tanker negligently allow oil to leak from their boat into Sydney Harbour. As the oil leaks it mixes with debris and spreads to the wharf owned by the claimants where a ship is undergoing welding repairs. Sparks from the welding activity ignite the oil and the fire damages the wharf and other ships nearby. It is known that thin oil on water is difficult to ignite. Should the owners of the tanker be responsible for all the damage? Would a reasonable person foresee that fire damage would be a direct consequence of the negligent oil spillage?

This is what the court had to consider in *Overseas Tankship (UK) Ltd v Morts Dock and Engineering Co (The Wagon Mound) No 1* [1961] AC 388 (PC). Prior to this case the court had considered that there was liability for all damage which was a physical consequence of the defendant's breach of duty, so that would mean the damaged wharf and boats. However, the court asked whether the kind of damage suffered by the claimant was reasonably foreseeable at the time that the breach of duty occurred. The court found that the oil spillage damaging the slipway was foreseeable (and therefore recoverable in damages) but that the substantial fire affecting the wharf and moored boats was unforeseeable (not recoverable in damages) due to oil being difficult to ignite on water.

Revision tip

When considering SQE1 questions relating to legal causation and remoteness of damage remember that if the *type* or *kind* of damage is foreseeable it does not matter that the extent of the damage is not foreseeable. So, for example, if the court had decided in *The Wagon Mound* that fire was in fact foreseeable, it would not matter that the fire destroyed one boat or one hundred boats, the defendants would have been liable for the whole extent of the damage.

Revision tip

When considering the possible cause of harm, list the possible causes and eliminate those which are not the factual cause of the harm, and then consider whether the harm suffered is not too remote.

Eggshell skull

When we consider any claims in negligence in SQE1, remember the **'eggshell skull theory'** dictates that we take our victims as we find them. It is no defence to a claim to state that the claimant has suffered damage due to their previous state of health. **Practice example 2.6** illustrates the eggshell skull theory.

Key term: eggshell skull theory

The eggshell skull theory means that the court will not allow the defendant to blame the claimant's pre-existing state of health for the consequences of the breach of duty suffered by the claimant.

Practice example 2.6

The claimant's lip is burnt following a splash of molten liquid during the course of his employment. The claimant suffers from a pre-cancerous skin condition. Due to the molten liquid injury he succumbs to cancer. Is the defendant employer liable for the type (the actual damage to his lip) and extent (cancer) of the damage?

This is what the court had to decide in *Smith v Leech Brain & Co Ltd* [1962] 2 QB 405 (CA). The court found that as long as the physical injury to the lip was foreseeable it did not matter that the claimant was more susceptible due to his pre-existing condition. The defendant was liable for the full extent of the harm.

The eggshell skull principle has also been extended to claims involving a claimant with lack of means. In *Lagden v O'Connor* [2004] 1 AC 1067 (HL) the defendant was liable for the cost of the claimant hiring (on credit) a replacement vehicle following a road traffic accident caused by the defendant's negligence which left the claimant without a vehicle. The claimant was 'impecunious' as he was unable to afford to pay in advance for a hire vehicle. The defendant was liable for the higher credit costs.

Intervening acts

We have so far considered the defendant's negligence and whether that was the factual and legal cause of the harm. When preparing for

SQE1, you should also consider whether a chain of events, which starts with the defendant's negligence, is broken by any intervening acts resulting in the defendant not being liable for the claimant's harm. We refer to this as the chain of causation and intervening acts ('**novus actus interveniens**') which break the chain can either be:

- the claimant's act
- a third party's act
- a separate/natural act.

Key term: novus actus interveniens

A novus actus interveniens is a new intervening act that breaks the chain of causation, meaning that the original defendant's negligent act is not the cause of the claimant's damage/loss.

When considering whether a new intervening act has broken the chain of causation remember that the intervening act must be entirely unreasonable. If it is a reasonably foreseeable consequence of the original defendant's negligent act then it will not break the chain of causation and the original defendant will be liable.

Table 2.3 illustrates how the courts have dealt with later acts and whether they are attributable to the first negligent act or whether they have broken the chain of causation.

Table 2.3: Intervening acts

Type of intervening act	Effect
The claimant's act:	
The claimant suffered a leg injury due to the defendant's negligence which left him with a weakened leg. When descending stairs his leg gave way, causing him to jump the remaining steps, and in doing so he fractured his ankle. *McKew v Holland & Hannen & Cubitts (Scotland) Ltd* [1969] 3 All ER 1621 (HL)	The claimant's act of descending steep stairs (lacking a handrail) without seeking assistance was enough to break the chain of causation and the defendant was not liable.

Intervening acts (continued)

Type of intervening act	Effect
A third party's act:	
The defendant caused a road traffic accident in a tunnel. The attending police inspector sent the claimant police officer on a motorbike against the flow of traffic to close the tunnel entrance (this was contrary to police standing orders). The claimant officer was injured when he collided with oncoming traffic. *Knightley v Johns* [1982] 1 WLR 349 (CA)	The court found that the police inspector had been negligent in giving orders to drive against the flow of traffic and as a result this broke the chain of causation. The defendant was not liable for the claimant's injuries.
A separate/natural act:	
The claimant's ship was damaged in a collision by the defendant's ship and underwent temporary repairs. The claimant's ship was further damaged in a storm on route to the US to undergo permanent repairs. *Carslogie Steamship Co Ltd v Royal Norwegian Government* [1952] AC 292 (HL)	The claimants sought to recover the cost of all the necessary repairs from the defendant. The court held that the storm was a new intervening act which broke the chain of causation and the claimants could only recover the cost of the damage from the original collision with the defendants.

■ KEY POINT CHECKLIST

This chapter has covered the following key knowledge points. You can use these to structure your revision around, making sure to recall the key details for each point, as covered in this chapter.

- Causation relates to the connection between the defendant's negligent act (breach of duty) and the claimant's loss/damage.
- Causation has two distinct elements, factual and legal causation.
- In simple, single cause cases the court will use the 'but for' test to establish whether the negligent act was the factual cause of the claimant's damage/loss.
- The exceptions to the 'but for' test relate to more complex cases where there are many potential causes of harm. For multiple potential

causes of harm, the court will look at whether the defendant's negligent act materially contributed to the harm. For multiple sufficient causes the court will hold the defendants jointly and severally liable.

- For claims involving mesothelioma the claimant can recover damages from all responsible persons who will be both jointly and severally liable.
- For claims relating to 'lost chance', if the lost chance is less than 50% then on balance of probabilities the court is unlikely to find for the claimant. If the question relates solely to clinical negligence a lost chance claim cannot form the basis of the claim.
- Legal causation relates to whether the negligent act was the legal cause of the claimant's harm. If the loss/damage is too remote the claimant will not be liable.
- Intervening acts will break the chain of causation
- The eggshell principle means that the court will take the claimant as they find them.

■ KEY TERMS AND CONCEPTS

- causation (**page 35**)
- test of remoteness (**page 45**)
- eggshell skull principle (**page 46**)
- novus actus interveniens (**page 47**)

■ SQE1-STYLE QUESTIONS

QUESTION 1

The claimant attends at a busy hospital A&E complaining of a severe headache, dizziness and blurred vision for a number of days. It is very busy and the doctor (newly qualified in his first day on duty) briefly examines him and is in the process of prescribing him painkillers for a migraine when he collapses and dies. Medical evidence shows that the claimant suffered a stroke.

What statement best describes the court's approach when considering whether the treatment provided by the hospital was negligent?

A. The court will take into consideration how busy the A&E department was when the claimant attended.

B. The court will take into consideration whether the doctor's care has fallen below the standard of care expected.

C. The court will take into consideration the training and experience of the treating doctor.

D. The court will take into consideration whether the claimant has contributed to his injuries.

E. The court will take into consideration whether a majority of medical professionals would have prescribed painkillers for a migraine.

QUESTION 2

A baby is born by emergency caesarean due to complications with labour. The doctor on duty failed to appreciate that the baby was in distress and delayed calling the surgical team to perform the caesarean. Following birth, the baby suffers seizures and is left with long-standing health issues affecting speech, sight and hearing. Medical evidence is unable to say with certainty what the cause of the baby's health issues are, but medical experts agree that there are potentially three causes (genetic, oxygen starvation and bacterial infection). The court finds that each of the three causes have an equal percentage chance of being causative of the harm/damage.

Which of the following is most likely to be the position the court will adopt when considering the doctor's liability?

A. The court is likely to find the doctor liable in negligence as he breached his duty when failing to order the caesarean earlier and that breach was causative of the baby's health issues.

B. The court is likely to find that although the doctor breached his duty, his negligent act was one of three potential causes of the baby's harm and on balance of probabilities causation cannot be established.

C. The court is likely to find that although there were competing causes of the baby's harm, on balance, the doctor's negligence was causative and as a consequence the claim against the doctor will succeed.

D. The court is likely to find that the two non-negligent potential causes of the baby's harm are intervening events that break the chain of causation.

E. The court is likely to find the doctor liable as the two non-negligent potential causes of the baby's harm did not break the chain of causation.

QUESTION 3

The claimant contracts mesothelioma caused by exposure to asbestos. During his working life he had four periods of employment when he was exposed to asbestos. He worked for the first company for ten years. He worked for the second company for ten years. The third period of employment was for ten years when he was self-employed. The fourth period of employment was for ten years with a local company which is now insolvent.

Which of the following statements best reflects the approach of the court in determining liability for the negligent exposure to asbestos?

A. The court will hold each employer 25% liable, meaning the claimant will have 25% of his damages reduced to reflect his period of self-employment.
B. The court will hold only those employers liable that are solvent at the time the claimant brings the claim, meaning the claimant will receive only 75% of any damages.
C. The court will find that all defendants are jointly and severally liable, meaning the claimant can bring a claim against any of the solvent employers and receive 100% of any damages.
D. The court will find that all defendants are jointly and severally liable, meaning the claimant can bring a claim against any of the employers but his damages will be reduced by 25% to reflect his period of self-employment.
E. The court will find that all defendants are jointly and severally liable, meaning the claimant can bring a claim against any of the employers but his damages will be reduced by 25% to reflect his period of self-employment and a further 25% to reflect that one company is insolvent.

QUESTION 4

The claimant is travelling on the motorway when she sees a stationary vehicle in the middle lane. She brings her vehicle to a stop at a safe distance behind the stationary vehicle and puts her hazard warning lights on. The car behind her (car A) fails to stop in time and collides with the rear of her car, causing damage and injury. The car behind car

A (car B) fails to stop in time and collides with the rear of car A pushing car A into the claimant's vehicle, causing damage and injury. The experts agree that the claimant's injuries and vehicle damage have been caused in equal proportion by the drivers of car A and car B.

Which of the following statements best represents the position of the court in response to the liability of the responsible drivers?

A. The court is likely to find that the driver of car A is 100% liable for the damage and injury caused to the claimant.
B. The court is likely to find that the driver of car B is 100% liable for the damage and injury caused to the claimant.
C. The court is likely to find the collision caused by the driver of car A to be an intervening act which breaks the chain of causation.
D. The court is likely to find the drivers of car A and car B proportionally liable for the damage and injury caused to the claimant.
E. The court is likely to find the collision caused by the driver of car B to be an intervening act which breaks the chain of causation.

QUESTION 5

The claimant suffers a longstanding injury to her left knee when she slips on uneven carpet on the steps of the defendant's department store. The defendant accepts that the carpet has been laid negligently and the injury to the claimant's knee caused due to their breach of duty. The medical evidence confirms that the claimant has been left with a weak knee. Some months later the claimant is walking down the high street and trips over an uneven paving stone the council have negligently failed to repair and severely reinjures her left knee, resulting in her mobility being impaired.

Which of the following statements best represents the position of the court in response to the liability of the defendant department store?

A. The court is likely to find that the department store is proportionally liable for the claimant's continuing knee symptoms together with the council.
B. The court is likely to find that the claimant's continuing knee injuries are a new intervening act which breaks the chain of causation.

C. The court is likely to find that the department store is liable for the claimant's continuing left knee mobility impairment.

D. The court is likely to find that the council's negligence does not break the chain of causation and the department store are liable for the claimant's left knee mobility impairment.

E. The court is likely to find that the council's negligence breaks the chain of causation and the department store are not liable for the claimant's left knee mobility impairment.

■ ANSWERS TO QUESTIONS

Answers to 'What do you know already?' questions at the start of the chapter

1) The 'but for' test is the general test used to determine whether the defendant's breach of duty was the factual cause of the claimant's harm/loss. You need to consider whether, but for the defendant's negligence, the claimant would have suffered the harm. If the claimant would have suffered the harm the defendant's negligent act is not the factual cause of the harm. If the claimant would not have suffered the harm but for the defendant's negligence, then the defendant's negligence is the factual cause of the claimant's harm and the defendant is liable.

2) The exceptions to the 'but for' test are:

   a) Multiple potential causes – where there is more than one cause of the claimant's harm, it is the defendant whose breach has materially contributed to or materially increased the risk/harm that will be liable.

   b) Multiple sufficient causes – where there is a later non-fault or natural event causing harm the defendant will be liable for the proportion of harm that but for their negligence the claimant would not have suffered. Remember that if the claim relates to mesothelioma the defendants causing the negligent exposure to asbestos will be jointly and severally liable.

   c) Lost chance – where the defendant's negligence has caused the claimant to lose the chance of a more favourable outcome. Remember the court is unlikely to impose liability where the claimant has lost the chance of avoiding injury/harm.

3) True – intervening acts will break the chain of causation.

4) The answer is (d) – a novus actus interveniens is a new intervening act that breaks the chain of causation, meaning that the original

defendant's negligent act is not the cause of the claimant's damage/loss.

5) The eggshell skull theory dictates that we take our victims as we find them. It is no defence to a claim to state that the claimant has suffered damage or loss due to the nature of their character or due to their previous state of health.

Answers to end-of-chapter SQE-style questions

Question 1:

The correct answer was B. This is because the doctor will be judged by the standard of care of a medical professional.

A is wrong because the standard of care is not affected by how busy the A&E department was when the claimant attended – a doctor owes a patient a duty of care.

C is wrong because experience is not taken into consideration. Irrespective of how long the doctor has been in the role the court will judge the doctor by the standard of care of a medical professional.

D is wrong because the court only considers the defence of contributory negligence when the defendant is found to be liable, but in any event the claimant has not contributed to his injuries.

E is wrong because the correct test is whether the doctor acted in accordance with the actions of a responsible body of medical opinion.

Question 2:

The correct answer was B. This is because the court is likely to find that although the doctor breached his duty, his negligent act was one of three potential causes of the baby's harm and on balance of probabilities causation cannot be established. The doctor's negligence is potentially only 33.33% causative and therefore does not meet the balance of probabilities burden of proof.

A is wrong because failing to order the caesarean earlier was only one of three possible causes of the baby's health issues.

C is wrong because the doctor's negligence is only 33.3% to blame for the baby's health issues and therefore causation cannot be established on the balance of probabilities.

D is wrong because the two other possible causes are not intervening events that break the chain of causation.

E is wrong because the three events are all possible causes and the chain of causation is not broken.

Question 3:

The correct answer was C. This is because the court will find that all defendants are jointly and severally liable, meaning the claimant can bring a claim against any of the solvent employers and receive 100% of any damages.

A is wrong because the employers are jointly and severally liable.

B is wrong because the claimant is entitled to bring a claim against any or all of the employers and receive 100% of the damages.

D is wrong because joint and several liability means that the claimant can claim against any of the responsible defendants and receive 100% of his damages.

E is wrong because the claimant is entitled to full damages from any of the responsible defendants.

Question 4:

The correct answer was D. This is because the drivers of car A and car B have caused equal damage and injury to the claimant and they are proportionally liable (50% each).

A is wrong because both cars A and B have equally (ie 50% each) caused the injury and damage to the claimant.

B is wrong because both cars A and B are responsible for the damage.

C is wrong because there is no intervening act but two collisions which were equally responsible for the claimant's injury and damage.

E is wrong because there is no intervening act which breaks the chain of causation.

Question 5:

The correct answer was E. This is because the council's negligence breaks the chain of causation and the department store will be liable only for the claimant's left knee symptoms which relate to the injury the claimant sustained when slipping on their uneven carpet. The council's negligence in failing to repair the pavement is the factual cause of the claimant's left knee mobility impairment.

A is wrong because the claimant's second accident breaks the chain of causation.

B is wrong because an event must occur to break the chain of causation and the claimant's continuing knee injuries are not a new intervening act.

C is wrong because the claimant suffers a further injury tripping in the street due to the council's negligence.

D is wrong because the second accident was due to the council's negligence and this causes the left knee mobility impairment.

■ KEY CASES, RULES, STATUTES AND INSTRUMENTS

You are not required to know case names for the purpose of SQE1 but it may be helpful to recall the names of the cases to assist with your revision:

- *Barnett v Chelsea and Kensington Hospital Management Committee* [1969] 1 QB 428 (QBD) ('but for' test)
- *Overseas Tankship (UK) Ltd v Morts Dock and Engineering Co (The Wagon Mound) No 1* [1961] AC 388 (PC) (Wagon Mound (No 1) (remoteness test)
- *Baker v Willoughby* [1970] AC 467 (HL) (novus actus interveniens)
- *Smith v Leech Brain & Co Ltd* [1962] 2 QB 405 (CA) (eggshell skull principle)

Negligence: Remedies, economic loss and psychiatric harm

■ MAKE SURE YOU KNOW

The previous chapters concentrated on the elements to be proved in establishing negligence. This chapter will concentrate on remedies in personal injury claims and the effect of psychiatric harm and economic loss. You are required to know the elements of negligence and apply the legal principles and rules appropriately and effectively to realistic client-based ethical problems and situations for your SQE1 assessment.

■ SQE ASSESSMENT ADVICE

As you work through this chapter, remember to pay particular attention in your revision to:
- the principles of remedies in personal injury and death claims
- the principles of establishing a claim for economic loss
- the principles of establishing a claim for psychiatric harm.

■ WHAT DO YOU KNOW ALREADY?

Have a go at these questions before reading this chapter. If you find some difficult or cannot remember the answers, make a note to look more closely at that during your revision.
1) What are the remedies for successful personal injury claims?
   [Remedies in personal injury and death claims, pages 58–61]
2) What are the remedies for fatal accident claims?
   [Remedies in personal injury and death claims, pages 58–61]
3) True or false?
   In respect of psychiatric harm claims, a primary victim must show that physical injury as a result of the defendant's negligence was reasonably foreseeable.
   [Claims for psychiatric harm, pages 65–70]

4) True or false?

In respect of psychiatric harm claims, a secondary victim must show that it was reasonably foreseeable for a person of reasonable fortitude to suffer some psychiatric injury.

[Claims for psychiatric harm, pages 65–70]

5) What does a claim for economic loss relate to?

a) Economic loss relates to non-financial loss which can be attributed to the physical harm caused by the defendant to the claimant or the claimant's property.

b) Economic loss relates to non-financial losses which cannot be attributed to the physical harm caused by the defendant to the claimant or the claimant's property.

c) Economic loss relates to financial losses which cannot be attributed to the physical harm caused by the defendant to the claimant or the claimant's property.

[Claims for economic loss, pages 61–65]

REMEDIES IN PERSONAL INJURY AND DEATH CLAIMS

Remedies in tort seek to put the claimant back into the position they would have been had the tort not occurred. In personal injury claims this is done by monetary compensation (damages) and, where the negligent act has caused the death of the claimant, their estate will claim damages on their behalf. Where the claimant is claiming damages for personal injury the claimant must bring the claim within three years from the date of the cause of action (ie, accident) or from the date the claimant had knowledge that the injury was due to the defendant's negligence. **Figure 3.1** lists the type of damages a successful claimant can expect to receive.

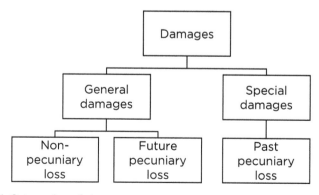

Figure 3.1: Categories of damage

Remedies for personal injury claims

Special damages compensate the claimant for all the financial (pecuniary) losses they have suffered prior to the trial of the action. General damages are split into two categories – *non-pecuniary* and *future pecuniary loss*. Non-pecuniary loss relates to compensation for the claimant's pain, suffering and loss of amenity. Future pecuniary loss relates to all financial losses the claimant will suffer over future years. **Table 3.1** gives examples of the main heads (categories) of damage in personal injury claims.

Table 3.1: Heads of damage

Type of damage	Examples
Special damages – past pecuniary loss	Loss of earnings
	Cost of medical care, aids and appliances
	Cost of transport, travel and accommodation
	Cost of damaged clothing and property
	Cost of DIY and gardening expenses
General damages – non-pecuniary loss	Damages for pain and suffering
	Damages for loss of amenity (enjoyment of life)
General damages – future pecuniary loss	Future loss of earnings
	Future cost of medical care, aids and appliances
	Future cost of transport, travel and accommodation
	Future loss of pension

Remedies for personal injury claims involving death

Where the claimant has died as a result of the negligent act prior to the trial, their estate can bring a claim for damages. **Figure 3.2** highlights the relevant legislation.

Law Reform (Miscellaneous Provisions) Act 1934

• allows the deceased claimant's estate to continue the claim

Fatal Accidents Act 1976

• allows a separate claim for the benefit of the deceased claimant's dependants

Figure 3.2: Damages in death claims

The Law Reform (Miscellaneous Provisions) Act 1934 (LR(MP)A 1934) allows the claim to continue for the benefit of the estate where the claimant has died. There is no need to bring a separate claim as the claim continues. The estate will be entitled to claim what the deceased was entitled to in the instant before he died. If the deceased claimant had no cause of action against the defendant, the deceased's estate will have no cause of action. Equally the defendant can use any defence they would have used against the claimant. Also, if the deceased claimant was contributory negligent the estate's damages will be reduced accordingly.

The Fatal Accidents Act 1976 (FAA 1976) allows a separate claim to be brought by the deceased claimant's dependants. The claim can only proceed if the claimant would have been able to sue successfully before he died. In order to bring a dependency claim under the Act, the claimant must be a 'dependant' as defined under the Act and must have had a reasonable expectation of financial benefit from the deceased. **Table 3.2** provides a list of dependants as defined under the FAA 1976.

Table 3.2: Statutory meaning of dependant

Dependant
Wife/husband – includes former wife/husband
Civil partner – includes former civil partner
Any person who: • was living with the deceased in the same household immediately before their death, and • had been living with the deceased in the same household for at least two years before that, and • was living during the whole period as husband/wife/civil partner of the deceased.
Any person treated by the deceased as his parent
Any child or other descendant of the deceased
Any person (not being a child of the deceased) who in the case of marriage was treated by the deceased as a child of the family in relation to that marriage
Any person (not being a child of the deceased) who in the case of any civil partnership was treated by the deceased as a child of the family in relation to that civil partnership
Any person who is, or is the issue of, a brother, sister, uncle or aunt of the deceased

Table 3.3 gives an overview of the possible heads of damage in death claims.

Table 3.3: Overview of damages in death claims

LR(MP)A 1934	FAA 1976
Pain, suffering and loss of amenity (up to date of death)	Bereavement award
Loss of earnings (up to date of death)	Dependency claim for dependants suffering financial losses
Care/services (up to date of death)	Funeral expense
Damage to personal property	Loss of consortium (personal affection of deceased)
Funeral expense	

CLAIMS FOR ECONOMIC LOSS

We have considered losses arising from negligent acts. **Figure 3.3** illustrates how these losses can be categorised.

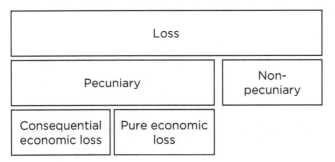

Figure 3.3: Loss in negligence

When considering the types of loss claimants suffer we can categorise losses as either non-pecuniary (not relating to money, eg pain and suffering) or pecuniary (relating to financial loss that can be proved and calculated). Pecuniary losses can also be split into **pure economic loss** and **consequential economic loss**. Generally, in tort, economic loss is not recoverable. **Practice example 3.1** illustrates a classic example of consequential economic loss and pure economic loss.

Key term: pure economic loss
Pure economic loss is financial loss resulting from the harm caused by the negligent act.

Key term: consequential economic loss

Consequential economic loss is financial loss sustained due to
another harm caused by negligence.

Practice example 3.1

The defendant's employees negligently damaged a cable supplying
electricity to the claimant's factory. As a result, the electricity board
shut off the electricity supply (for 14 hours) whilst the cable was
repaired. The claimants were unable to use their steel furnace and
had to dispose of the steel in the furnace. The claimants claimed
for (i) the damage to the steel disposed of, (ii) the lost profit from
selling the steel that had to be disposed of and (iii) the anticipated
loss of profit on the steel that could not be processed in the 14 hours
without electricity. Was the defendant responsible for all heads of
loss? Which are consequential and which are pure economic loss?

This is what the court had to consider in *Spartan Steel & Alloys Ltd v
Martin & Co (Contractors) Ltd* [1973] 1 QB 27 (CA). The court found
that (i) was physical damage to property and recoverable in tort,
that (ii) was consequential economic loss due to the damage to
property and recoverable in tort. The court concluded that (iii) was
pure economic loss and although incurred due to the defendant's
negligence was not a consequence of the damage to the property.

Revision tip

When considering questions dealing with consequential and
economic loss remember that pure economic loss, which is not
as a consequence of physical damage to property or harm to the
claimant, is not recoverable. Examples of pure economic loss could
be losses relating to trade, profits or revenue. However consequential
loss as a result of physical damage to property or harm to the
claimant will be recoverable. Examples of consequential loss are
property damage, personal injury or lost earnings.

We have seen that economic loss caused by a direct consequence of
physical damage is the exception to the general rule that economic loss
is not recoverable. The courts have also considered whether economic
loss is recoverable when suffered due to defective property or products.
The latest position is reflected in the classic case in **Practice example 3.2**.

Practice example 3.2

The council approved plans submitted by a housing development company to construct a concrete raft as a foundation for houses. Construction cracks appeared in the properties and it was established that the raft had subsided. The claimant sold his property at a loss of £35,000 and sued the council for economic loss. The claimant had no contractual relationship with the council. Is the council liable for the claimant's loss of £35,000 on the sale price on the basis that they approved defective plans?

This is what the court had to consider in *Murphy v Brentwood District Council* [1991] 1 AC 398 (HL). The court decided that the claimant could only recover the cost of repairing the defective building, not the economic loss incurred due to a reduction in the sale price of the property. The court found that the council had a statutory duty to approve the plans and inspect the property to ensure compliance with planning law but that did not create a duty of care covering economic loss.

Negligent misstatements

Claims in negligence suggest that a defendant has acted or failed to act. However, tort law recognises that in limited situations liability for negligent misstatements exists. **Practice example 3.3** illustrates the classic case which introduced this principle.

Practice example 3.3

The defendant was a bank which was asked to prepare a credit reference for a company the claimant's advertising company had been commissioned to work for. The company commissioning the claimants later went into liquidation owing the claimants £17,000. The claimant sued the bank on the basis that they had negligently prepared a statement as to the company's trustworthiness and credit. Did the bank owe a duty of care to the advertising company and could the claimant recover the loss on the basis of the negligent misstatement?

This is what the court had to consider in *Hedley Byrne & Co Ltd v Heller and Partners Ltd* [1964] AC 465 (HL). The bank had written a disclaimer stating that no liability could arise; however, the court found that in certain circumstances a duty of care could arise even where the harm was pure economic loss. The court restricted this principle to four situations:

a) where a special relationship of trust/confidence existed between the parties
b) where the party preparing the statement has voluntarily assumed the risk (either expressly or impliedly)
c) where there has been a reliance on the information/statement
d) where reliance on the statement was reasonable in the circumstances.

Table 3.4 illustrates cases where the court has considered these exceptions to the rule that pure economic loss is not recoverable in tort. Remember, when considering SQE1 questions, that there may be some situations where the court will allow a claim for economic loss.

Table 3.4: Examples of Hedley Byrne exceptions

Exception	Example case
Special relationship	Esso was found to owe a duty of care for pure economic loss when their employee negligently advised the claimant purchasing one of Esso's petrol stations that the output was higher than it actually was, thus causing the claimant to suffer economic loss due to reduced sales. *Esso Petroleum Co Ltd v Mardon* [1975] CA
Voluntary assumption of risk	Barclays Bank were obliged to freeze the accounts of companies in debt following court orders obtained by Customs and Excise. Barclays negligently allowed payments to leave the account. The court found that there had been no voluntary assumption of responsibility on behalf of Barclays as they were legally obliged to accept the freezing order and accordingly Customs and Excise could not recover the money (economic loss). *Customs & Excise Commissioners v Barclay Bank* [2007] 1 AC 181
Reliance	It was acknowledged that a house buyer would place reliance upon a survey obtained by the mortgage company to ensure the property is worth the amount they are seeking to borrow, even though no contract exists between house buyer and surveyor. *Smith v Eric S Bush* [1990] 1 AC 831 (HL)

Examples of Hedley Byrne exceptions (continued)

Exception	Example case
Reliance reasonable in circumstances	Reliance upon auditors' accounts relating to a company which was ultimately found to be worthless was unreasonable. Company accounts are a requirement under the Companies Act 1985 and not for potential investors to use as a measure of whether the company is worth investing in. *Caparo Industries plc v Dickman* [1990] 2 AC 605 (HL)

CLAIMS FOR PSYCHIATRIC HARM

In order to bring a claim for **psychiatric harm** the psychiatric injury must be medically diagnosed (by a medical expert) and recognised. **Figure 3.4** illustrates how the court have classified different conditions.

Key term: psychiatric harm

Psychiatric harm in a legal context means a recognised psychiatric illness caused by a sudden shock or horrifying event. It is more than grief, sorrow or sadness.

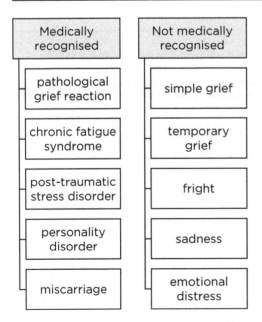

Figure 3.4: Psychiatric conditions

To successfully claim for psychiatric harm the claimant must fall into the category of either a **primary victim** or a **secondary victim**. The two categories were established in the landmark case of *Alcock v Chief Constable of South Yorkshire Police* [1992] 1 AC 310. The case involved claims brought by the families of victims of the Hillsborough football stadium disaster. The defendants allowed a large number of spectators into a crowded stand (with a perimeter fence) in the stadium, causing 96 spectators to be crushed to death. Claims were brought by victims' family members, some of whom were present or witnessed the event on television.

Primary victims

Primary victims are normally involved in the accident. A primary victim must show that physical injury as a result of the defendant's negligence was reasonably foreseeable. Primary victims are owed a duty of care in respect of psychiatric harm as long as they can establish that physical injury was foreseeable. They do not need to show that psychiatric harm was foreseeable.

Key term: primary victim

A primary victim is one that is in the physical zone of danger or reasonably believes that they are in danger.

Practice example 3.4 illustrates a case brought by a primary victim.

Practice example 3.4

The claimant was involved in a car accident with the defendant's vehicle, but he suffered no physical injury. He did, however, suffer a relapse of myalgic encephalomyelitis (ME) from which he was in remission. Did the defendant owe the claimant a duty of care as a participant in the accident?

This is what the court had to consider in *Smith v Page* [1996] AC 155 (HL). The court found that it was foreseeable that the claimant could have suffered a physical injury due to the fact he was in the zone of physical danger. Due to this, the fact that he had suffered psychiatric harm was sufficient to bring him into the scope of the defendant's duty of care. The court held that the eggshell skull principle (see Chapter 2) applied and the claimant's predisposal to psychiatric harm was of no consequence.

Secondary victims

Secondary victims are normally bystanders to the event and will not have suffered any physical injury but may have suffered psychologically due to witnessing the incident. Secondary victims have to show that it was reasonably foreseeable for a person of reasonable fortitude to suffer some psychiatric injury. They must also satisfy the test (control mechanisms) laid down in *Alcock* as follows:

a) the class of persons recognised (must have a close tie of love and affection)

b) closeness of the claimant (in time and space to the aftermath)

c) the means by which the shock is caused (witnessed with own unaided senses).

Key term: secondary victim

A secondary victim is one that is not within the physical zone of danger and will not have suffered physical harm.

Table 3.5 illustrates examples of each of these mechanisms.

Key term: Alcock control mechanism

The *Alcock* control mechanism is the test the court uses to ascertain whether there is a duty of care owed in cases involving psychiatric injury.

Table 3.5: Secondary victims: Alcock control mechanism

Control mechanism	Example
Close tie of love and affection	Rebuttable presumption in favour of parents, children and spouses, but other cases must be proved. Claimant at the ground who witnessed the death of his two brothers failed as he could not prove a close tie to the two brothers. *Alcock v Chief Constable of South Yorkshire Police* [1992] 1 AC 310
Closeness in time and space to aftermath	Claims brought by relatives (not present at ground) identifying bodies of their families some 8–9 hours post incident failed as were not part of the aftermath. *Alcock v Chief Constable of South Yorkshire Police* [1992] 1 AC 310

Secondary victims: Alcock control mechanism (continued)

Control mechanism	Example
Means by which shock witnessed	Family members watching the events of the Hillsborough stadium disaster unfold on television were unable to claim as secondary victims as they did not witness the event or the immediate aftermath with their own unaided senses. *Alcock v Chief Constable of South Yorkshire Police* [1992] 1 AC 310

Revision tip

When dealing with SQE1 questions about (medically diagnosed) psychiatric harm, first consider whether the claimant is a primary victim by considering whether they were in the zone of physical danger – remember, the eggshell skull principle applies to primary victims. Secondly, consider whether the claimant was a secondary victim using the *Alcock* test mechanism. Remember, secondary victims must show that some psychiatric harm was reasonably foreseeable in a person of reasonable fortitude.

Further categories

We have looked at psychiatric harm and how the courts deal with cases. There are some categories of claimants where the distinction between primary and secondary victims causes difficulty. These are considered below.

Rescuers

Rescuers who attempt to assist victims of accidents are neither primary nor secondary victims. They are not in the zone of physical danger and would not fulfil the *Alcock* test mechanism. **Practice example 3.5** explains the classic case illustrating the principle.

Practice example 3.5

Police officers attempting to rescue victims of the Hillsborough disaster suffered psychiatric harm as a result of what they witnessed. Claims were brought by three police officers on duty at the ground (two were positioned in the morgue and one had tried to help the victims over the perimeter fence), two police officers who arrived later in the day and witnessed the upsetting scenes, and one officer who was sent to a local hospital to liaise with families of the victims. The claimants did not meet the requirements of either primary or secondary victims. Did their employers owe them a duty of care as rescuers or employees?

This is what the Court had to consider in the case of *White and others v Chief Constable of the South Yorkshire Police* [1999] 2 AC 455 (HL). The court refused to extend the categories of primary or secondary victim to include rescuers. As such, rescuers would only be primary victims if they found themselves exposed to physical danger.

Destruction of property

The court has indicated that a claimant could recover damages for psychiatric illness following witnessing the destruction of property. In *Attia v British Gas plc* [1988] QB 304 (CA), the claimant had suffered nervous shock as a result of witnessing fire damage to her property following the negligent installation of a central heating system by the defendants. The court held that a person could recover damages if they were able to prove causation and reasonable foreseeability.

Anxiety/Future disease

The court have held that damages for anxiety related to potential risk of future disease are not recoverable. In *Rothwell v Chemical & Insulating Co Ltd* [2007] 3 WLR 876 (HL) the claimant was negligently exposed to asbestos and developed pleural plaques. He suffered anxiety due to the potential risk of future disease. The court held that the law did not recognise a duty of care to take reasonable care not to cause anxiety and that the defendants could not have reasonably foreseen psychiatric illness to be a consequence of their breach of duty years before.

Involuntary involvement

The courts have considered claims brought by unwilling participants in other people's deaths or injury. Prior to *Alcock*, the court had allowed recovery of damages related to psychiatric illness suffered by the claimant as a result of the fear that they had caused the death of someone else. In order for a claim to succeed, there has to be a reasonably held belief that the claimant has been involuntarily involved in another's death or injury. The court considered a claim for psychiatric illness brought by the claimant who was responsible for installing a platform in *Monk v PC Harrington* [2008] EWHC 1879 (QB). The platform collapsed following the negligence of a crane operator, killing a worker. The court did not accept that the claimant reasonably believed he had caused the accident (as there was no evidence to suggest this) but that the claimant had feelings of guilt. Further, that the claimant's attempt to help following the collapse did not place the claimant in fear of his own safety and so the claim failed.

Assumption of responsibility

The court has held that in certain relationships a defendant assumes responsibility to ensure that the claimant is not exposed to reasonably foreseeable psychiatric harm. Examples of these relationships are employer/employee, doctor/patient and police/police informant. **Practice example 3.6** illustrates an example of where the assumption of responsibility was found between prison officers and prisoners.

Practice example 3.6

The claimant who suffered with depression was placed in a cell with a suicidal prisoner. The suicidal prisoner went on to commit suicide and the claimant suffered severe shock. Did the prison officers owe a duty of care to prevent a prisoner, who they knew to suffer with depression, suffering psychiatric harm in placing him in a cell with a suicidal prisoner?

This is what the court had to consider in *Butchart v Home Office* [2006] EWCA Civ 239. The court held that the defendant knew or ought to have known that the claimant was vulnerable to psychiatric harm and that they owed a duty of care to take reasonable steps to minimise the risk of the claimant suffering psychiatric harm, which in the circumstances extended to not placing him in a cell with a suicidal prisoner.

■ KEY POINT CHECKLIST

This chapter has covered the following key knowledge points. You can use these to structure your revision around, making sure to recall the key details for each point, as covered in this chapter.

- Remedies in tort seek to put the claimant back into the position they would have been had the tort not occurred. Compensation is awarded in personal injury claims. Where the negligent act has caused the death of the claimant, their estate will claim damages on their behalf.
- Damages can be classified as pecuniary loss (money related) and non-pecuniary loss (non money related).

- Generally, in tort, economic loss is not recoverable, but there are exceptions to the rule.
- In order to bring a claim for psychiatric harm, the psychiatric injury must be medically diagnosed and only victims falling into primary or secondary victim categories may recover damages.

■ KEY TERMS AND CONCEPTS

- pure economic loss (**page 61**)
- consequential economic loss (**page 62**)
- psychiatric harm (**page 65**)
- primary victim (**page 66**)
- secondary victim (**page 67**)
- *Alcock* test mechanism (**page 67**)

■ SQE1-STYLE QUESTIONS

QUESTION 1

The claimant suffers severe head injuries following a serious road traffic accident. She works full time and is married with two young children and her wife works part time. The claimant is placed in a surgical coma but never resumes consciousness and dies three weeks after the accident. The driver of the other vehicle confirms pulling out of a junction without checking the road and admits liability for the accident.

Which of the following is likely to be the position in respect of a claim for compensation on behalf of the claimant and her family?

A. The claimant's estate can continue the claim which the deceased was entitled to in the instant before dying and the deceased's dependents can bring a separate dependency claim as the claimant would have been able to sue the defendant successfully.

B. As the claimant is deceased, all claims come to an end unless the claimant gave permission for the claim to be pursued prior to her death.

C. The claimant's estate can bring a claim but the deceased's relatives would not be able to bring a claim as the deceased was not entitled to claim in the instant before dying.

D. The claimant's estate can continue the claim but there can be no separate dependency claim as the claimant did not gain consciousness before her death.

E. The claimant's estate and dependants are unable to bring a claim as the claimant would have been unable to sue successfully prior to death.

QUESTION 2

The claimant is injured in an accident at work when he falls from scaffolding which has been negligently erected by his employer. He suffers severe head injuries and is taken to hospital where he dies several hours later. His employers have admitted liability for the accident. The claimant was a single father and financially supported his 19-year-old son through university. The claimant left his estate to his son.

Which statement accurately reflects whether the son will be able to bring a dependency claim?

A. The claimant's son is unable to bring a dependency claim as the claimant was unlikely to receive compensation for his injuries.

B. The claimant's son will be able to bring a dependency claim only if he is able to show that the claimant suffered pain and suffering from the date of the accident until the date of death.

C. The claimant's son is unable to bring a dependency claim as the claimant is deceased and all claims come to an end unless the claimant gave permission for the claim to be pursued prior to his death.

D. The claimant's son will be able to bring a dependency claim as a child of the deceased with a reasonable expectation of financial benefit from the deceased.

E. The claimant's son is unable to bring a dependency claim as the son is an adult over the age of 18 and dependency claims are only available to children of the deceased.

QUESTION 3

A food production company specialising in ice cream production suffers a power outage at their factory due to the local electricity supplier's employee negligently severing a cable in the junction box outside the factory during some regular maintenance work. The food production company pursues a claim in negligence against the electricity supply company and liability is admitted for the negligent breach of duty. Due to the break in supply of electricity, the food production company lose the current batch being pasteurised (batch product), losing £500, and the packed end product in the freezing operation (frozen product), losing a further £1,000. Had the electricity supply not been cut, the production company would have made a further 75% profits on the raw mix ingredients waiting to go through the food process. The raw mix ingredients had to be disposed of.

Which of the following is likely to be the position the court will adopt when considering what the food production company can claim in respect of their losses?

A. The court is likely to allow a claim for damages for the batch product, the frozen product and the 75% lost profits as all were consequential on the electricity supplier's negligent act.

B. The court is likely to allow a claim for damages for the batch product, the frozen product and the 75% lost profits as the batch and frozen products were consequential on the electricity supplier's negligent act and the 75% lost profits are economic loss but recoverable due to the defective nature of the production equipment caused by the electricity supplier's negligence.

C. The court is likely to dismiss the claim for damages for the batch product, the frozen product and the 75% lost profits as none were consequential on the electricity supplier's negligent act.

D. The court is likely to allow a claim for damages for the batch product and the frozen product as the damage to the batch and frozen products were physical damage but dismiss the claim for 75% lost profits on the mix ingredients as this further loss of profit is pure economic loss and not recoverable.

E. The court is likely to dismiss a claim for damages for the batch product, the frozen product and the 75% lost profits as they are not a consequence of physical damage and are all pure economic loss and not recoverable.

QUESTION 4

The claimant suffers from severe depression and an associated personality disorder after viewing the news on his phone on route to work. The news article shows viral videos from the internet of a train derailment in Wales. The footage of the train crash shows passengers being thrown out of the train and the scene of devastation. The cause of the train derailment was the negligent signalling failure of the rail company. The claimant's mother and daughter were on the train and were seriously injured but have since recovered.

Which of the following statements best reflects the approach of the court in respect of a claim for psychiatric injury brought on behalf of the claimant?

A. The court will likely conclude that severe depression and a personality disorder are not medically recognised psychiatric disorders and the claimant will be unable to claim damages in negligence against the rail company.

B. The court will likely conclude that the claimant is not a primary victim, as the claimant was not in the zone of physical danger, but is a secondary victim as the claimant is likely to have a close tie of love and affection with both his mother and daughter.

C. The court will likely conclude that the claimant is neither a primary nor secondary victim as the claimant was not in the zone of physical danger and did not witness the aftermath with his own unaided senses due to viewing it on the internet.

D. The court will likely conclude that the claimant is not a primary victim as he was not in the zone of physical danger but is a secondary victim as the scene was one of devastation.

E. The court will likely conclude that severe depression and a personality disorder are medically recognised psychiatric disorders and the claimant will be able to claim damages in negligence against the rail company.

QUESTION 5

The claimant is a police officer on duty when she is called to the scene of a live music concert where many in the audience have suffered breathing difficulties due to carbon monoxide poisoning. The concert organisers had negligently allowed the concert to go ahead despite being advised by an engineer called out to service the concert hall's boiler that there was a fault on the boiler. Many concert goers were unable to leave the concert due to a fire door being bolted shut and have succumbed to the fumes and died. The claimant is severely affected by the sight of dead bodies and suffers clinical depression, causing her to remain off work for six months.

Which of the following statements best represents the position of the court in respect of a claim for psychiatric injury brought by the claimant police officer?

A. The court is likely to conclude that the claimant has suffered a medically diagnosed psychiatric illness and award her damages for psychiatric harm.

B. The court is likely to conclude that clinical depression is not a medically diagnosed psychiatric illness and the claim for damages for psychiatric harm will fail.
C. The court is likely to conclude that the claimant is a rescuer and will award damages for psychiatric harm.
D. The court is likely to conclude that the claimant is neither primary nor secondary victim and the claim for damages for psychiatric harm will fail.
E. The court is likely to conclude that the claimant is a secondary victim and award damages for psychiatric harm.

■ ANSWERS TO QUESTIONS

Answers to 'What do you know already?' questions at the start of the chapter

1) The remedies for a successful personal injury claim are damages (pecuniary and non-pecuniary).
2) The remedies for fatal accident claims under LR(MP)A 1934 allow the claim the deceased was entitled to in the instant before dying to continue for the benefit of his estate. FAA 1976 allows a separate claim to be brought by the deceased claimant's dependants. The claim can only proceed if, before he died, the claimant would have been able to sue successfully.
3) True. In respect of claims for psychiatric harm, primary victims are normally involved in the accident. A primary victim must show that physical injury as a result of the defendant's negligence was reasonably foreseeable.
4) True. Secondary victims are normally bystanders to the event and will not have suffered any physical injury but may have suffered psychologically due to witnessing the incident. Secondary victims have to show that it was reasonably foreseeable for a person of reasonable fortitude to suffer some psychiatric injury.
5) The answer is (c). Economic loss relates to financial losses which cannot be attributed to the physical harm caused by the defendant to the claimant or the claimant's property. Remember the exception to this is where the economic loss suffered is as a consequence of physical damage to the claimant's property.

Answers to end-of-chapter SQE1-style questions

Question 1:

The answer was A. The claimant's estate can continue the claim which will be based on the losses the claimant would have been entitled to prior to her death. A separate claim by the deceased's dependants can also be brought which will include a dependency claim, an award for bereavement damages and (if paid) a claim for funeral expenses.

B is wrong because the claim does not come to an end just because the claimant dies before they are able to receive an award of compensation.

C is wrong because the claimant's estate would be able to bring a claim.

D is wrong because it is not a condition that the claimant must survive any length of time in order to bring a claim.

E is wrong because the claimant would have been able to successfully sue the driver of the vehicle as the driver was negligent in pulling out of the junction and driving into the claimant's car.

Question 2:

The answer was D. This is because the deceased claimant's son will be able to bring a claim as he is a dependant and being financially supported by the claimant whilst at university.

A is wrong because the claimant would receive compensation for his injuries as the claimant's employers were negligent.

B is wrong because there is no requirement to show that the claimant suffered pain from the date of the accident until death.

C is wrong because the claim does not discontinue just because the claimant has died, as the estate is able to continue with the claim.

E is wrong because there is no cut-off point in respect of age.

Question 3:

The answer was D. This is because economic loss which is a direct consequence of physical damage is an exception to the rule that economic loss is not recoverable. So, the £1,500 loss made on the batch and frozen product is pure economic loss and is recoverable. The loss of 75% profits on the raw mixture which had to be thrown away is not due to damage to property and is not recoverable.

A is wrong because the damage to the batch product and the frozen product is a direct consequence of physical damage and this falls into the exception to the rule that economic loss is not recoverable. The claimant would be able to recover damages for the batch and frozen product. However, 75% loss of profits on the raw material that had to be thrown away was not a direct consequence of physical damage

B is wrong because the 75% profits on the batch wasted due to the power cut is not attributable to the damage to the claimant's property caused by the defendant's negligence. The profits on the wasted product are pure economic loss and do not fall into the exception (economic loss which is a direct consequence of physical damage).

C is wrong because the batch product and the frozen product were damaged due to the defendant's negligence and fall under the exception to the rule that economic loss is not recoverable.

E is wrong because losses associated with the batch and frozen product (£1,500) are economic loss which fall into the exception to the rule as they are as a direct consequence of the physical damage to the claimant's property and the court will award £1,500 in compensation. The 75% profit loss has not been incurred due to a direct consequence of the physical damage to the claimant's property.

Question 4:

The answer was C. This is because the claimant was not a primary victim (in zone of physical danger) and did not witness the aftermath with his own unaided senses (a requirement for a secondary victim).

A is wrong because even though severe depression and personality disorders are medically recognised psychiatric disorders, which is a requirement to claim for psychiatric harm, the claimant does not fulfil the criteria of either primary or secondary victim.

B is wrong because, although the court will conclude that the claimant is not a primary victim (in the zone of physical danger), he is not a secondary victim as he did not witness the aftermath with his own unaided senses (a requirement for a secondary victim).

D is wrong because the claimant is not a primary victim and does not qualify as a secondary victim (close tie of love and affection, closeness in time and space to aftermath and witnessed with own unaided senses).

E is wrong because, although the claimant's injuries are medically recognised psychiatric disorders, the claimant does not satisfy the test for a primary or secondary victim.

Question 5:

The answer was D. This is because the police officer is neither a primary nor secondary victim which is a requirement to claim damages for psychiatric harm. She will be unable to recover damages for psychiatric harm.

A is wrong because, although the claimant has suffered a medically diagnosed psychiatric illness, she does not fall into the primary or secondary victim category.

B is wrong because clinical depression is a medically diagnosed psychiatric illness, but the claim will fail as the claimant is neither a primary nor secondary victim.

C is wrong because the claimant would have to be either a primary or secondary victim to claim successfully.

E is wrong because the claimant is not a secondary victim.

■ KEY CASES, RULES, STATUTES AND INSTRUMENTS

The SQE1 Assessment Specification does not require you to know case names, but this case contains important principles which are worth remembering:

• *Alcock v Chief Constable of South Yorkshire Police* [1992] 1 AC 310

4

Defences

■ MAKE SURE YOU KNOW

Previous chapters concentrated on the requirements in establishing negligence. This chapter concentrates on the defences available to the defendant when faced with a claim in negligence. You are required to know the defences to negligence and apply the legal principles and rules appropriately and effectively to realistic client-based ethical problems and situations for your SQE1 assessment.

■ SQE ASSESSMENT ADVICE

As you work through this chapter, remember to pay particular attention in your revision to:
• when and to what extent the defences are available
• whether the defence is absolute or partial
• whether the defence is applicable to all torts or a special category
• specific categories of claimants.

■ WHAT DO YOU KNOW ALREADY?

Have a go at these questions before reading this chapter. If you find some difficult or cannot remember the answers, make a note to look more closely at that during your revision.
1) What defences are available to the defendant faced with a claim in negligence?
   [Defences, page 80]
2) What two elements must the defendant prove in citing consent as a defence?
   [Consent, pages 81–83]
3) True or false?
   The defence of 'illegality' is a complete defence to a claim in negligence.
   [Illegality, pages 87–88]

4) In raising a defence of contributory negligence which issue is *not* considered by the court?
    a) whether the claimant failed to exercise reasonable care for their own safety
    b) by what percentage should the claimant's damages be reduced
    c) whether the defendant contributed to the claimant's harm
    d) whether the failure to exercise reasonable care contributed to the claimant's harm
    [Contributory negligence, pages 84–87]
5) What effect does the Law Reform (Contributory Negligence) Act 1945 have on the claimant's damages if successfully pleaded?
    [Contributory negligence, page 84]

DEFENCES

Most claims in negligence are defended on the basis that the defendant did not owe the claimant a duty of care, or that if a duty was owed it was not breached. Further, that if the duty was breached, that the negligence was not factually or legally causative of the harm suffered. Where the claimant has established negligence there are three general defences available to a defendant. There are also specific defences available for particular torts. We will concentrate on the three general defences in this chapter and we will deal with the defences to specific torts in the relevant chapters (**Chapter 6** and **Chapter 8**). The three general defences are illustrated in **Figure 4.1**.

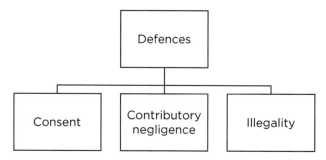

Figure 4.1: Defences

CONSENT (VOLENTI NON FIT INJURIA)

The defence of consent (**volenti non fit injuria**) relates to the concept that the claimant has consented to the activity which carried a risk of harm and should not be able to blame the defendant when that risk causes harm or damage. If successfully pleaded, it is a complete defence and the defendant will not be liable for the harm/damage. In order to establish the defence of consent, there are two necessary elements the defendant must prove: first, that the claimant had full knowledge of the nature and extent of the risk involved and second, that the claimant voluntarily accepted the risk – see **Figure 4.2**.

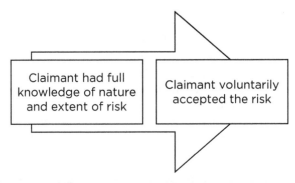

Figure 4.2: Necessary elements to successfully plead the defence of consent

Key term: volenti non fit injuria

Volenti non fit injuria is Latin for 'there can be no injury to one who consents'.

Knowledge

The claimant must have knowledge of the risk and agree to it. The test is a subjective one and it is not enough just to be aware of the risk – the claimant has to accept it. **Practice example 4.1** illustrates the principle in practice.

Practice example 4.1

The claimant spends an afternoon drinking with a friend. The friend drinks over half a bottle of whisky and they both decide to take the friend's light aircraft for a ride. The aircraft crashes, killing the friend piloting the aircraft and leaving the claimant seriously injured. Had the claimant consented to the nature and extent of the harm by accompanying his friend who was drunk?

This is what the court had to consider in *Morris v Murray* [1991] 2 QB 6 (CA). They found that the incident was '*a drunken escapade, heavily fraught with danger*' (Fox LJ). The court held that the claimant was not so drunk as to not appreciate the extent and nature of the risk but had accepted and agreed to the risk knowing that the friend was so drunk that he was unable to fly the aircraft competently.

Voluntary acceptance of risk

The claimant must have freely accepted the risk. Having knowledge of a risk is not the same as consenting to it. Consider that instead of agreeing to go for a ride in the defendant's aircraft in *Morris* the claimant had openly expressed that it was a bad idea and tried to convince the defendant not to take the plane out but felt obliged to accompany him. It is likely that the claimant would have defeated the defendant's (estate) defence of consent. Although the claimant had knowledge of the risk associated with flying an aircraft whilst drunk, the court would accept that he has not voluntarily accepted the risk if he was objecting to the defendant's actions.

Revision tip

Remember that, in order to freely accept the risk, the claimant must be able to consent. Therefore, a child or someone detained under the Mental Capacity Act 2005 is unable to consent as they cannot freely accept the risk.

The court have considered particular claimants and the issue of consent. **Table 4.1** looks at how the courts have dealt with these particular categories of claimants.

Table 4.1: Consent and specific claimants

Category	Treatment
Passengers: Injured in vehicles driven by a defendant under the influence of alcohol where they are aware that the defendant is drunk – can they consent to any injury caused by the defendant's negligent driving?	Section 149 of the Road Traffic Act 1988 excludes consent as a defence to a claim in negligence. The court may, however, reduce the claimant's damages to reflect contributory negligence.

Consent and specific claimants (continued)

Category	Treatment
Employees: Injured undertaking work they know to carry significant risk of harm – can they consent to the risk of injury?	In *Smith v Charles Baker Sons* [1891] AC 325 (HL), the claimant was injured when a stone fell from a crane close to where he was working on the railway. The court held that even though the claimant continued in employment with full knowledge of the risk it did not mean the defendant could argue consent. The common law duty of care afforded to employees would also mean that the defendant should be aware of any risks to their employees and protect them accordingly.
Involvement in sporting activities: Those injured whilst taking part in sporting activity voluntarily – can they consent to any associated injury they sustain?	In *Condon v Basi* 1985 1 WLR 866 (CA) the claimant suffered a broken leg following a foul tackle by the defendant. The court held that the claimant's consent did not extend to the injury which had been inflicted by the defendant in breach of his duty of care. Whilst those participating in sporting activities can be said to consent, for example, to be tackled playing football, participants cannot be said to consent to foul play that would extend to a serious injury.
Those injured whilst spectating sporting activities – can they consent to the risk of harm associated with watching the sport?	In *Wooldridge v Sumner* [1963] 2 QB 43 (CA) the claimant (photographer) was injured at a horse race when the defendant made an error of judgement and took a corner too fast. The court held that the claimant had consented to the risk of damage caused by an error of judgement or lapse of skill. Whilst spectators can be said to consent to a lapse of skill, they would not be expected to consent to reckless disregard for spectators' safety (eg a negligent act).

CONTRIBUTORY NEGLIGENCE

If the claimant has contributed to the harm or damage that they are claiming the defendant's negligence has caused, the court may make a finding of **contributory negligence**. The attention is on the injuries and the extent that the claimant contributed to their own injuries (not the extent the claimant contributed to the accident). Contributory negligence is not a complete defence. The Law Reform (Contributory Negligence) Act 1945 allows the court to have regard to the claimant's share in the responsibility of the damage. If the court make a finding of contributory negligence, they will reduce the claimant's damages to reflect the claimant's negligence. In order to rely on the defence, the court will consider the following:

• whether the claimant failed to exercise reasonable care for their own safety
• whether this failure contributed to the claimant's damage
• to what extent the claimant's damages should be reduced.

Key term: contributory negligence

Contributory negligence relates to the claimant's failure to take reasonable care of their own safety and as a result the claimant will be found to have contributed to the damage/harm they are claiming the defendant has caused.

Table 4.2 considers the elements the court will consider when faced with a defence of contributory negligence.

Table 4.2: Contributory negligence: court's considerations

Considered element	Example case
Failure to exercise reasonable care for their own safety: The court will consider what a reasonable person could have done to avoid being hurt.	In *Jones v Livox Quarries Ltd* [1952] 2 QB 608 (CA) the claimant was injured whilst riding on the back of a vehicle in contravention of his employer's instructions. The court found that the claimant had not acted as a reasonable prudent man and he should have foreseen he might hurt himself. The court reduced his damages by 20%.

Contributory negligence: court's considerations (continued)

Considered element	Example case
Contribution to claimant's damage: The court will consider whether the claimant's carelessness had an effect on the injury.	In *Rickson v Bhatar* [2017] EWHC 264 (QBD) the claimant cyclist suffered severe injuries during a timed trial bike race when he collided with the defendant's van as it turned across his path. The court found that the claimant did not slow down (possibly due to his head down position and not observing the van) but did swerve at the last minute. The court reduced the claimant's damages by 20% to reflect the claimant's contribution to the injury.
Extent to which damages should be reduced: The court will consider to what extent the claimant's behaviour caused or contributed to the injuries. Also, What the culpability (blameworthiness) of the claimant is.	In *Froom v Butcher* [1976] QB 286 (CA) the claimant (passenger) who was not wearing her seatbelt was injured when the defendant's vehicle collided with her vehicle. The court used a sliding scale to calculate the percentage reduction in damages to reflect the non-wearing of a seatbelt: a) Injuries prevented – 25% reduction b) Injuries less severe – 10% reduction c) No difference – 0% reduction. The *Froom* guidelines are also applicable to accidents involving motorcycles and bicycles.

Exam warning

Remember when considering SQE1 questions relating to contributory negligence that the 1945 Act specifies that contributory negligence can be used as a defence to other torts, not just negligence. It is the most common defence cited in tort claims.

Special claimants

The court may consider different factors for some claimants when considering whether they could have contributed to their injury. In assessing contributory negligence in relation to negligence claims the court will never make a finding of 100% contributory negligence. **Table 4.3** highlights examples of how the courts have dealt with different categories of claimants where the claimants have contributed to their injuries.

Table 4.3: Examples of contributory negligence

Claimant type	Example case
Children: The younger the child the less likely the court will make a finding of contributory negligence. Generally, children under 10 years old will not be held to be contributory negligent.	Contributory negligence cases involving children are often road traffic accidents where the child(ren) run into the path of a driver in an attempt to cross the road. In *Gough v Thorne* [1966] 1 WLR 1387 guidance was given by the court: 'A judge should only find a child contributory negligent if he or she is of such an age to be expected to take precautions for his or her safety' (Lord Denning). The court also found that the child must be 'blameworthy'. In *Gul v McDonagh* [2021] EWHC 97 (QB) a 13-year-old was held 10% contributory negligent for crossing the road without observing the defendant's vehicle (which was driven with excess speed).
Employees: Where an employee is injured at work the court will assess the claimant's conduct and working conditions. Reckless disregard for an employer's rules by an employee is more likely to lead to a finding of contributory negligence.	In *Eyres v Atkinsons Kitchens & Bathrooms* [2007] EWCA Civ 365 the claimant was driving home after working long hours for his employer, the defendant (who was asleep in the front seat), when he crashed his vehicle. The court found the claimant 33.3% contributory negligent on the basis that he had to bear some responsibility for his injuries.
Rescuers: Where a rescuer has rushed to assist in an emergency situation caused by the defendant's negligence the rescuer's actions will be judged by the standards of a reasonable rescuer. Courts are reluctant to 'punish' rescuers.	In *Baker v TE Hopkins & Sons Ltd* [1959] 1 WLR 966 (CA) the claimant was a doctor who died attempting to rescue the defendant's workers who were overcome by fumes from a well (which they were warned to stay away from). The court found no contributory negligence on the part of the rescuing doctor. The court found that only if the rescuer had taken wholly unreasonable disregard for their own safety would a finding of contributory negligence be relevant.

Exam warning

When considering SQE1 questions regarding a defendant's
negligence, consider whether the claimant's behaviour has
contributed to his injuries. Contributory negligence does not
completely defeat a claim but if the court finds the claimant
contributed to the harm by failing to take care of their own safety
the court will reduce the claimant's damages.

Illegality (ex turpi causa non oritur actio)

The defence of illegality, or **ex turpi causa non oritur actio**, relates to
the concept that it would be against public policy to allow someone to
benefit from undertaking an unlawful act. Illegality is a complete defence
to a claim and if successfully pleaded the claimant will not receive any
damages. For example, consider the situation if a burglar is injured as
they trip on a defective step leaving a block of flats they have broken
into. It would be against public policy to allow the burglar to succeed in
a civil claim (negligence) against the owner of the flats. The burglar is
undertaking criminal activity and should not be able to benefit from a
civil claim.

Key term: ex turpi causa non oritur actio

Ex turpi causa non oritur actio is Latin for 'from a dishonourable
cause an action does not arise'.

For the defence to succeed there needs to be a connection between the
illegal activity and the injury suffered by the claimant. In the example
above, if instead of tripping down the stairs the burglar had been run
over by a car on their route home, the driver of the car would not be
able to claim the defence of illegality as there is no real connection
between the road traffic accident injuries sustained by the burglar and
the committing of the burglary. The burglary has not caused the road
traffic accident.

The courts have reached different decisions in considering whether to
allow the defence of illegality to succeed. **Table 4.4** gives an insight
into how the courts have dealt with the defence of illegality pleaded in
response to claimants that have been injured whilst involved in illegal
activity.

Table 4.4: Examples of illegality defences considered by the courts

Example of illegal activity	How the courts reacted
The claimant, a pillion passenger, knowing the defendant was drunk, underage and uninsured, encouraged him to drive recklessly. The defendant was killed in the subsequent accident and the claimant seriously injured.	The court found that both were engaged in an illegal act and as a result found that there was no duty of care between them. The claimant's claim was defeated by the defence of illegality. *Pitts v Hunt* [1991] 1 QB 24 (CA)
The claimant was injured when he jumped from his flat window in the course of being pursued to be arrested by police officers.	The court found that the police officer did not have a duty of care to prevent the claimant from injuring himself whilst trying to evade custody. The claimant's claim was defeated by the defence of illegality. *Vellino v Chief Constable of Greater Manchester Police* [2002] 1 WLR 218 (CA)
The claimant was a passenger in a vehicle found to be supplying drugs prior to being pursued by the police and suffered injuries when the vehicle collided with oncoming traffic in an attempt to evade the police car.	The court found that the likelihood of a collision was foreseeable and that the claimant had been part of a joint enterprise to supply drugs. The claimant's claim was defeated by the defence of illegality. *Blake v Croasdale* [2018] EWHC 1919 (QB)
The claimant was shot and injured by the defendant lying in wait with a shotgun in his shed following a reported increase in burglaries.	The court found that the defendant's actions of lying in wait for burglars with a shotgun was disproportionate and the defence of illegality failed. The claimant recovered damages for injury (these were reduced by two-thirds to reflect the claimant's contributory negligence). *Revill v Newberry* [1996] QB 567 (CA)

Revision tip

When revising remember that some defences are general (consent, illegality, contributory negligence) and they can apply to all torts and that some are specific and apply only to particular torts (warning notices – occupier's liability, prescription, necessity – nuisance).

■ KEY POINT CHECKLIST

This chapter has covered the following key knowledge points. You can use these to structure your revision around, making sure to recall the key details for each point, as covered in this chapter.

- Once the claimant has proved negligence (duty, breach, causation and loss) the only possibility available to the defendant to attempt to defeat the claim is to successfully defend it.
- The defence of consent and illegality are complete defences to negligence and if accepted by the court the claimant will not receive damages.
- In order to successfully defend a claim on the basis of consent, the defendant must show that the claimant had full knowledge of the extent and nature of the risk and willingly accepted it.
- In order to successfully defend a claim on the basis of illegality, the defendant must show that there is a connection between the illegal act and the injury suffered by the claimant.
- Contributory negligence is a partial defence to a negligence claim.
- In order to successfully defend a claim on the basis that the claimant contributed to their injuries, the defendant must prove that the claimant's behaviour has caused or contributed to the claimant's injuries.

■ KEY TERMS AND CONCEPTS

- volenti non fit injuria (**page 81**)
- contributory negligence (**page 84**)
- ex turpi causa non oritur actio (**page 87**)

■ SQE1-STYLE QUESTIONS

QUESTION 1

The claimant, a five-year-old child who is accompanied to an ice cream van with his father, is knocked over as he goes around the front of the ice cream van and walks into the defendant's vehicle. The defendant's vehicle was travelling at a speed of 25mph. The area is a built-up residential area and there is a queue of children on the pavement waiting to be served.

Which of the following is likely to be the position of the court when considering the defendant's argument that the claimant contributed

to his injuries by failing to take reasonable care of his own safety when crossing the road?

A. The court is likely to find that the claimant has contributed to his injuries by failing to take care of his own safety and reduce his damages by 10%.

B. The court is likely to find that the claimant has contributed to his injuries by failing to take care of his own safety and reduce his damages by 25%.

C. The court is likely to find that the claimant has contributed to his injuries by failing to take care of his own safety and reduce his damages by 50%.

D. The court is likely to find that the defendant's speed was excessive to pass an ice cream van in a residential area and the defence of contributory negligence will fail.

E. The court is likely to find that the child's father is contributory negligent and reduce the claimant's damages accordingly.

QUESTION 2

The claimant, lying drunk in the road of a cul-de-sac, is injured when the defendant's vehicle reverses over him late at night. The defendant is looking over his right shoulder and reverses for 40 feet before reaching and reversing over the claimant. It is accepted that if the defendant had looked over his left shoulder at any point he would have seen the claimant lying in the road.

Which of the following is likely to be the position of the court when considering the defendant's argument that the claimant contributed 100% towards his injuries by getting drunk and lying in the road?

A. The court is likely to find the claimant 100% contributory negligent for his injuries and reduce his damages to zero.

B. The court is likely to find that liability will attach to the defendant for failing to look over his left shoulder but that the claimant has contributed to his injuries by being drunk and lying in the road and reduce his damages accordingly.

C. The court is likely to find the defendant not at fault for the accident.

D. The court is likely to allow the defence of illegality to succeed due to the claimant being drunk in a public place.

E. The court is likely to allow the defence of consent to succeed on the basis that the claimant consented to being a victim of a road traffic accident by lying in the road when drunk.

QUESTION 3

The claimant is playing rugby which is refereed by a part-time amateur referee when the scrum he is participating in collapses, causing him serious neck injuries. The evidence accepted by the court is that had the referee adhered to the rules and sequence of engagement during the game the scrum would not have collapsed.

Which of the following is likely to be the court's approach to the defendant's attempts at defending the claim?

A. The court will likely accept that the referee breached his duty by failing to prevent a scrum collapse and that the defendant's defence, based on the fact that the claimant consented to his injuries by accepting the risk involved in rugby, will fail.

B. The court will likely accept that the referee breached his duty by failing to prevent a scrum collapse but that the defendant's defence, based on the fact that the claimant consented to his injuries by accepting the risk involved in rugby, will succeed.

C. The court will likely accept that the referee owed a duty of care but that, by the very nature of the sport of rugby, it is to be expected that injury will occur and that the referee did not breach this duty of care, allowing a complete defence to the claimant's claim.

D. The court will likely accept that the referee breached his duty by failing to prevent a scrum collapse but allow a reduction in damages to reflect the claimant's contributory negligence by actively taking part in the scrum.

E. The court will likely allow a partial defence of consent on the basis that the claimant consented to all risks involved in the sport.

QUESTION 4

The claimant parks her car on double yellow lines in a no-parking zone when the defendant drives into a collision with the claimant's vehicle, causing extensive damage.

Which of the following is likely to be the court's approach to the defendant's argument in his defence that the claim should be defeated on the basis of the illegality of the claimant's parking?

A. The court is likely to allow the defendant to defend the claim on the basis of illegality as there was a connection between the claimant's parking and the damage inflicted by the defendant's driving.

B. The court is unlikely to allow the defendant to defend the claim on the basis of illegality but reduce the claimant's damages significantly to reflect that she had parked in a no-parking zone.

C. The court is unlikely to allow a defence of illegality but may allow a defence of consent on the basis that the claimant voluntarily accepted the risk of someone driving into her vehicle whilst parked illegally.

D. The court will not allow the defence of illegality as the claimant's positioning of her vehicle is not an important factor and does not contribute to the damage to the vehicle.

E. The court will not allow the defence of illegality but is likely to find the claimant 100% contributory negligent and reduce the claimant's damages to zero.

QUESTION 5

The claimant is a front seat passenger in her brother's car which is involved in a road traffic accident when the defendant changes lanes on the motorway. The defendant admits that he failed to see the vehicle the claimant was travelling in. The claimant, who was not wearing a seatbelt at the time of the accident, is seriously injured. The court accepts that had she been wearing a seatbelt her injuries would have been less severe.

Which statement best represents the court's approach in dealing with the claimant's contribution to her injuries?

A. The court is unlikely to make a finding of contributory negligence as the claimant has not contributed to the accident.

B. The court is unlikely to make a finding of contributory negligence as the claimant has not contributed to her injuries.

C. The court is likely to make a finding of 10% contributory negligence as the claimant has contributed to her injuries by failing to wear a seat belt.

D. The court is likely to make a finding of 25% contributory negligence as the claimant has contributed to her injuries by failing to wear a seat belt.

E. The court is likely to reduce the claimant's damages by 50% to reflect she was not wearing a seat belt.

■ ANSWERS TO QUESTIONS

Answers to 'What do you know already?' questions at the start of the chapter

1) Consent, illegality and contributory negligence.
2) The claimant had full knowledge of the risk and voluntarily accepted the risk.
3) True – it is a complete defence.
4) The answer is (c) as the court will consider whether there is a duty, breach and whether the breach was causative. If they find the defendant was negligent they will then consider any defence the defendant has raised. They will not consider whether the defendant has contributed as the court has already established that the defendant is liable.
5) The Act allows the claimant's damages to be reduced and is reflected in the percentage by which the claimant has contributed to their injuries.

Answers to end-of-chapter SQE1-style questions

Question 1:
   The correct answer was D. This is because the area is residential and an ice cream van is parked on the road. The court will likely find that the claimant should have taken more care when driving and should have foreseen children crossing near the ice cream van.

   A, B and C are wrong because the court are unlikely to reduce the damages of a child; the defendant would need to defend the claim on the basis that the father contributed to the child's injuries by failing to stop the child crossing the road.

   E is wrong because children crossing near the ice cream van should be anticipated by motorists. Had the defendant been driving at an appropriate speed (eg 5mph) he may have been able to avoid the accident. A speed of 25mph is too fast in the circumstances and the court will likely find him wholly to blame for the claimant's injuries.

Question 2:
   The correct answer was B. This is because the onus is always on a reversing driver to ensure that the road is clear and the fact that had the defendant looked over their left shoulder they would have seen the claimant in the road means the court will find the defendant at

fault but reduce the claimant's damages to reflect the fact that their behaviour contributed to the injuries. This example is based on a real claim and the court found the claimant 60% to blame, reducing the claimant's damages by 60%.

A is wrong because there cannot be a finding of 100% contributory negligence.

C is wrong because had the claimant not got drunk and fallen asleep in the road they would not have been injured. The claimant has to bear some responsibility for his injuries.

D is wrong because it is not illegal to get drunk and sleep in the road, just inadvisable.

E is wrong because the claimant did not consent to being a victim of a road traffic accident – he just carelessly fell asleep in the road.

Question 3:

The correct answer was A. This is because the claimant consented only to the normal risks involved in playing rugby, not the injury caused when the referee did not meet the required standard of care in refereeing the match.

B is wrong because the claimant consented only to the normal risks involved in playing rugby, not being injured due to the referee falling under the required standard of care.

C is wrong because, although rugby is a physical sport and injuries are commonplace, the referee's standard of care fell below that expected and this was the reason the claimant was injured.

D is wrong because the claimant's actions did not contribute to his injuries.

E is wrong because the claimant did not consent to injuries caused by the negligence of the referee.

Question 4:

The correct answer was D. This is because in order for a defence of illegality to succeed there needs to be a connection between the illegal activity and the harm caused. The fact the claimant had parked on double yellow lines is trivial. The defendant should have observed the road and has breached his duty to drive to the standard of a reasonably careful driver and observed her parked vehicle.

A is wrong because parking on double yellow lines is not a criminal offence.

B is wrong because the claimant has caused the accident by driving into the claimant's stationary vehicle.

C is wrong because the claimant's vehicle (although parked in contravention of the parking restrictions) was there to be seen and the defendant has failed to observe the presence of the vehicle on the road and caused the accident.

E is wrong because the court will not make a finding of 100% contributory negligent.

Question 5:

The correct answer was C. This is because the court will make a finding of 10% contributory negligence as the claimant's injuries would have been less severe had she worn a seat belt.

A is wrong because contributory negligence focuses on the claimant's contribution to her injuries, not her contribution to the accident.

B is wrong because the claimant has contributed to her injuries by failing to wear a seatbelt.

D is wrong because the court will make a finding of 25% contributory negligence only where the claimant's injuries would have been prevented entirely.

E is wrong because the court would only reduce a claimant's damages by 50% if the claimant was equally to blame for their injuries and the claimant does not have the same culpability as the defendant driver.

■ KEY CASES, RULES, STATUTES AND INSTRUMENTS

The SQE1 Assessment Specification does not require you to know any case names for the topic but you may find it useful to be familiar with:

• Law Reform (Contributory Negligence) Act 1945

5

Vicarious liability and employers' liability

■ MAKE SURE YOU KNOW

This chapter will cover principles of vicarious liability and employers' liability. You are required to know the principles of vicarious liability and employers' primary liability, including the operation and effect of the common law principles, and apply the legal principles and rules appropriately and effectively to realistic client-based ethical problems and situations for your SQE1 assessment.

■ SQE ASSESSMENT ADVICE

As you work through this chapter, remember to pay particular attention in your revision to:
• the steps required in establishing vicarious liability
• the principles of establishing a claim at common law against an employer.

■ WHAT DO YOU KNOW ALREADY?

Have a go at these questions before reading this chapter. If you find some difficult or cannot remember the answers, make a note to look more closely at that during your revision.

1) True or false?

A defendant will only be vicariously liable if there is an employee/ employer relationship between the defendant and the person committing the tort.

[Vicarious liability, pages 97–103]

2) What is the economic reality test?

[Vicarious liability, pages 97–103]

3) Complete the missing words.

Employers are under a duty to take reasonable care of their employees and liability will arise when employees are injured by a failure to take such care as per the common law principles. The common law principles relate to _____, _____ _____ and _____.

[Employers' liability, pages 103–105]

4) True or false?

An employer will be vicariously liable for the negligent acts of an independent contractor.

[Employers' liability, pages 103–105]

VICARIOUS LIABILITY

Vicarious liability is the principle by which a person may be held liable for the actions of a third party because of the relationship between the two parties. It can be applied to most torts and relies upon the relationship between the defendant and the person (third party) that commits the tort. It can be applied in different scenarios but is usually encountered in employer/employee relationships. In practice if an employer is vicariously liable for the negligence of their employee, the claimant can sue either employer or employee as they are jointly liable. The employee is primarily liable for the negligent act but the employer has secondary liability due to the relationship between employer and employee. In order to establish vicarious liability three elements must be present. **Figure 5.1** illustrates the essential requirements to show vicarious liability relating to an employer/employee relationship.

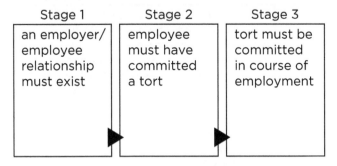

Stage 1	Stage 2	Stage 3
an employer/ employee relationship must exist	employee must have committed a tort	tort must be committed in course of employment

Figure 5.1: Elements of vicarious liability

Key term: vicarious liability

Vicarious liability is the principle which dictates that someone other than the third party that carried out the negligent act will be liable for the claimant's injury.

Employer/employee relationship

An employer will be held vicariously liable for the torts of an employee but not those of an independent contractor. The courts use a variety of tests to establish whether the person is an employee or an independent contractor. **Table 5.1** illustrates how the courts have dealt with distinguishing these relationships.

Table 5.1: Tests utilised in vicarious liability cases

Test	Case
Control test Does the employer have the right to control the individual? If so, the individual is likely to be in a relationship of employee/employer.	An employee is likely to work under the supervision and direction of an employer whilst an independent contractor is his own master. *Performing Right Society, Limited v Mitchell and Booker (Palais de Danse) Limited* [1924] 1 KB 762
Integral test Is the individual integral to the business or just an accessory to it? If the individual is integral they are more likely to be an employee.	There is a distinction between a contract of services (employee) and a contract for services (independent contractor). Under a contract of services the person is more likely to be integral to the business and under a contract for services the person is not integral but an accessory to the business. *Stevenson Jordan & Harrison Ltd v MacDonald & Evans* [1952] 1 TLR 101 (CA)
Economic reality test Where the control and integral test offer no solution, the economic reality test can be used.	There are three conditions that have to be fulfilled in order for a worker to be considered an employee: a) the employee in return for a wage provides work or skill for the employer b) the employee agrees (expressly or impliedly) that they will work under the control of the employer c) the other provisions of the contract are consistent with it being a contract of employment. *Ready Mixed Concrete Ltd v Minister of Pensions* [1968] 2 QB 497 (DC)

Revision tip

When considering questions dealing with vicarious liability think about the circumstances of the employment. Employees tend to be paid weekly or monthly, have tax and national insurance contributions deducted at source, and have fixed hours of work. Independent contractors normally receive one-off payment for jobs, are responsible for their own tax and national insurance and have more control over their working hours.

The test which the courts use to impose vicarious liability between employer and employee relates to whether it is fair, just and reasonable to impose vicarious liability as follows:
• The employer is more likely to have the means to compensate the victim than the employee and can be expected to have insured against that liability.
• The tort will have been committed as a result of activity being taken by the employee on behalf of the employer.
• The employee's activity is likely to be part of the business activity of the employer.
• The employer, by employing the employee to carry on the activity, will have created the risk of the tort committed by the employee.
• The employee will to a greater or lesser degree have been under the control of the employer. (*Catholic Child Welfare Society v Various Claimants* [2012] UKSC 56.)

An employer has a non-delegable duty of care which means that the employer cannot delegate his duty of care to a third party. Although an employer will not be vicariously liable for the negligent acts of an independent contractor, they may be found liable for harm suffered at the hands of that independent contractor if the employer has breached their duty of care to their employees.

Employee must have committed a tort
There can be no vicarious/secondary liability without direct/primary liability, so if the employee has not committed a tort the employer cannot be vicariously liable for their actions. Vicarious liability may apply to all torts but is commonly associated with negligence. Employers have been found vicariously liable for sexual assault, harassment and battery committed by their employees.

Tort must be committed in the course of employment
An employer will only be responsible for a tort committed by an employee in the course of their employment. If the court judge the employee to have deviated from the job they are employed to carry out they may conclude that the employee is on a 'frolic of their own' and the employer

will not be vicariously liable for their actions. The court has accepted that the following are in the course of employment:

a) authorised acts of the employee

b) authorised acts carried out in an unauthorised manner.

Authorised acts

If the employee commits a tort whilst carrying out an authorised act for his employer, the employer will be vicariously liable for that tort. For example, a security guard physically detaining individuals and preventing them from leaving premises could be committing the tort of battery and false imprisonment. Here the employer would be vicariously liable for the battery and false imprisonment, as detaining suspected shoplifters falls within the authorised activity of a security guard.

Authorised act carried out in an unauthorised manner

Issues have arisen where employees have carried out their work in an unauthorised manner. This may mean that the employee does what is asked of them but does so in a negligent manner. They will usually be found to be acting within the course of their employment. **Practice example 5.1** illustrates an example of this.

Practice example 5.1

A petrol tanker driver is employed to transport and deliver petrol. During delivery of the petrol to the oil tank the driver lit a cigarette and threw the match on the ground, causing the petrol to explode. Was the driver acting in the course of his employment?

This is what the court had to consider in *Century Insurance v NI Road Transport Board* [1942] AC 509 (HL). The court found that the driver was acting in the course of his employment as he was completing an authorised act (petrol delivery) in an unauthorised manner (whilst smoking).

There is a distinction between carrying out authorised acts in an unauthorised manner and an employee acting outside the scope of their employment. If found to be acting outside the scope of employment the employer is unlikely to be held vicariously liable for the employee's acts/omissions. When considering Practice example 5.1, envisage that the petrol tanker driver is employed only to transport the petrol and a second employee is employed to dispense the petrol delivery. If the driver decides to dispense the petrol as the second employee has gone for lunch, and in doing so negligently floods the customer's forecourt, causing a customer to slip and sustain injury, it is likely that the employer will not be vicariously liable for the driver's act as he was acting outside the course of his employment. He is employed only to drive not to dispense petrol.

Prohibited acts

What falls within and outside the scope of the course of employment has been tested many times in the courts. The court has distinguished between the manner (how to do the job) and the scope (what the employee should do). If an employee is prohibited from a certain activity but when he carries it out it furthers his employer's business, the court is more likely to find this falls within the course of employment. Employees acting in a prohibited manner may not always fall outside the course of their employment, as seen in *Century Insurance*. **Practice example 5.2** provides an example of this distinction.

Practice example 5.2

A milkman, despite being expressly prohibited to allow others to assist in the delivery of milk, allows a 13-year-old child to ride on the milk float and deliver milk. The child falls off the milk float due to the milkman's negligent driving. Can the child recover damages from the milkman's employers on the basis that they are vicariously liable for the milkman's negligence?

This is what the court had to consider in *Rose v Plenty* [1976] 1 WLR 141 (CA). The court found that the prohibition in allowing others to assist only affected the conduct of the employment (how to do the job). It did not define or limit the scope of his duties (what the employee should do). The disregard of his employers' instructions was a wrongful performance of how to do the job but it was not for his own purposes and did not take the activity outside of the scope of his duties (what he should do). The employer was vicariously liable for the milkman's negligence.

Consider that, instead of the milkman allowing a 13-year-old child to assist him delivering milk in *Rose*, the milkman allows the 13-year-old and his friends to ride on the milk float and gives them a lift to school, again injuring them due to negligent driving. The prohibition on allowing others to assist affects the conduct of the employment – how to do the job. In giving the children a lift the milkman's activity is outside the scope of what he should do and would fall outside the scope of his employment. He is not employed to give children lifts on the milk float. In that situation the court is likely to find the employer not vicariously liable for the milkman's negligence.

Unlawful acts

We have seen that even a prohibited act could be deemed to be in the course of employment depending on the facts of the case. Unlawful or criminal acts have also been considered by the court. For example, in *Lister and Others v Hesley Hall Ltd* [2002] 1 AC 215 (HL) the court used a 'close connection' test. The defendant employed wardens at a school for children with behavioural difficulties, one of whom sexually abused children in his care. The court considered that there was a close connection between the unlawful act and the employment as the abuse occurred on the employer's premises whilst the employee was carrying out his duties of caring for the children.

In considering the close connection test the court will look at the link between the unlawful act and the activities the employee should have been carrying out. Consider **Practice example 5.3** and how the court used the test.

Practice example 5.3

A customer at a petrol station forecourt approached one of the employees and asked if he could print off documents from a USB stick. The employee refused and used aggressive and racist language. The employee followed the claimant as he returned to his vehicle and violently attacked him. Was the defendant's employer vicariously liable for the attack?

This is what the court had to consider in *Mohamud v WM Morrison Supermarkets* [2016] UKSC 11. The court used the close connection test set out in *Lister* and found that the employee's duties were to deal with enquiries and customers. The verbal abuse was within the 'field of activities' that the job involved. Further, the unprovoked attack was part of the sequence of events and a seamless episode from the verbal abuse. The employers were found to be vicariously liable for their employee's attack.

Indemnity

If an employer is found vicariously liable for the negligence of their employee, they are both liable (**joint tortfeasors**); this means that the employer may recover the cost of damages from the employee. Under common law the court has allowed recovery from the employee where the injury is due to the employee's breach of contract. Under statute the employer could bring a claim for a contribution to any damages paid to the claimant under the Civil Liability (Contribution) Act 1978. The court will consider each case on its facts but, where an employer is blameless, they may order the employee to pay the whole damages if just and equitable. **Practice example 5.4** provides an example of this principle.

Key term: joint tortfeasors

A tortfeasor is the person responsible for committing or carrying out the tort. A joint tortfeasor relates to the fact that there may be more than one person responsible for committing the tort and causing harm or damage to the claimant.

Practice example 5.4

An employee, during the course of his employment, allows his father to accompany him to collect waste products in the employer's lorry. When reversing the lorry, the employee injures his father. The employee's father brings a claim for personal injury against his son's employers. The court finds the employers vicariously liable for their employee's negligence and awards the father damages. Is the employer entitled to recoup damages from the employee?

This is what the court had to consider in *Lister v Romford Ice & Cold Storage Co Ltd* [1957] AC 555 (HL). The court considered that the employee owed a duty to their employer to complete their duties with reasonable care in the driving and management of the vehicle. In failing to drive with care and skill, the employee had breached this duty and any compensation awarded by the court to the father could be recouped from the (employee) son.

Employers' liability

All employers have both statutory and common law duties to ensure their employees' safety. Following the Enterprise and Regulatory Reform Act 2013, the right to bring a civil action for breach of the statutory health and safety legislation was removed. The SQE1 specification requires only that you know the operation and effect of the common law principles in respect of **employers' liability**. We will therefore concentrate on common law principles.

Key term: employers' liability

Employers' liability relates to the duty at both common and statutory law an employer has in respect of their employees.

Common law duty of care

The duty to take reasonable care of employees' health and safety in the course of their employment rests with an employer. The employer cannot

delegate or pass this duty to another. The duty to take reasonable care was explained in *Wilsons & Clyde Coal Co Ltd v English* [1983] AC 57 (HL). An employer is expected to provide:
- competent staff
- adequate plant and equipment
- a safe system of work
- safe premises.

Exam warning

The court imposes a duty to take reasonable care – it is not an absolute or strict duty. When considering questions involving accidents at work, the outcome in respect of liability will very much depend on the facts of the case and what the court considers is reasonable in the circumstances.

Table 5.2 explains the duty of care and illustrates cases where the courts have considered these common law duties.

Table 5.2: Employers' common law duty of care

Common law duty of care	Example case
Competent staff An employer is vicariously liable for employee's negligence.	An employer will be liable for their employee's incompetence if they knew or ought to have known about their employee's behaviour. In *Hudson v Ridge Manufacturing Co* [1957] 2 QB 348 the court found the employer liable for injuries suffered following one employee tripping another. The employee had a history of practical jokes which the employer should have been aware of.
Adequate plant and equipment Plant means anything used in the course of work. An employer is under a duty to take reasonable steps to provide and maintain adequate plant and equipment.	Equipment includes any article of whatever kind furnished by the employer for the purposes of his business. In *Knowles v Liverpool County Council* [1993] 1 WLR 1428 (HL) the claimant was injured when a flagstone with a manufacturing defect broke as he carried it. The court held that the employer was liable for any defects that were not visible or obvious under the 1969 Act. The employer will be liable only if the defective equipment caused the claimant's injury.

Employers' common law duty of care (continued)

Common law duty of care	Example case
The common law duty is also supplemented by the Provision and Use of Work Equipment Regulations (1998) and the Employer's Liability Defective Equipment Act (1969)	In *McWilliam v Sir William Arrol & Co Ltd* [1962] 1 WLR 295 (HL) the claimant (steel erector) fell to his death as he was not provided with safety equipment. However, it was accepted he would not have worn the harness even if provided and, as such, although in breach, the defendant was not liable.
A safe system of work The duty to provide a safe system of work is very wide and includes: • ensuring systems and safety measures are complied with • warning staff about risks and dangers and guarding against them.	Safe system of work includes the physical layout of the job, the sequence in which work is carried out, the provision of warnings, notices and special instructions, and whether the system needs to be modified or improved. In *Speed v Thomas Swift & Co Ltd* [1943] 1 KB 557 (CA) the claimant was injured during the loading of a ship. The loading had been carried out taking into account previous damage to the ship, which prevented a safer method of loading. The court found that, in view of the special circumstances, the system of work should have been modified to take into consideration the special circumstances.
Safe premises The duty applies to the employer's premises and third-party premises where employees are expected to work and includes consideration of the: • place of work • nature of the building • experience of the employee • nature of the work • degree of control exercised by employer • employer's knowledge of the premises. The common law duty is also supplemented by the Workplace (Health, Safety and Welfare) Regulations 1992.	The duty is to take reasonable care to ensure the employee is not injured by the state of the premises. In *Latimer v AEC Ltd* [1953] AC 643 (HL) the claimant slipped on the factory floor which had flooded. The employer had used sawdust but had run out before the whole of the floor could be covered. The court held that the employer had done what was reasonable and was not liable.

■ KEY POINT CHECKLIST

This chapter has covered the following key knowledge points. You can use these to structure your revision around, making sure to recall the key details for each point, as covered in this chapter.

• The elements required in establishing whether the defendant is vicariously liable for the acts or omissions of a third party are: an employer/employee relationship must exist, the employee must have committed a tort, and the tort must have been committed in the course of employment.

• The tests used by the courts in establishing vicarious liability are the control test, the integral test and the economic reality test.

• Employers are under a duty to take reasonable care of their employees and liability will arise when employees are injured by a failure to take such care as per the common law principles.

• At common law, an employer is under a duty to provide safe premises, safe plant, materials and equipment, a safe system of work and competent staff.

■ KEY TERMS AND CONCEPTS

• vicarious liability **(page 97)**
• joint tortfeasors **(page 103)**
• employers' liability **(page 103)**

■ SQE1-STYLE QUESTIONS

QUESTION 1

The claimant is a catering manager at a local prison and is injured by a prisoner she is supervising when the prisoner loses his balance and drops a large pack of rice he was attempting to unload into the kitchen. The bag of rice falls onto the claimant's back. The prisoner receives payment for assisting in the kitchen.

Which of the following is likely to be the position of the court when considering whether the prison is vicariously liable for the negligence of the prisoner?

A. The court is unlikely to find that the prison is vicariously liable for the prisoner's negligence as he is not an employee but a prisoner.

B. The court is unlikely to find that the prison is vicariously liable for the prisoner's negligence as there is no close connection between the prisoner's negligence and the lack of supervision.

C. The court is unlikely to find that the prison is vicariously liable for the prisoner's negligence as there is no element of control between the supervisor and the prisoner.

D. The court is likely to find that the prison is vicariously liable for the prisoner's negligence as the prisoner is working as an integral part of the operation of the prison.

E. The court is likely to find that the prison is vicariously liable for the prisoner's negligence but reduce damages to reflect that the prisoner did not intentionally drop the pack of rice.

QUESTION 2

The claimant suffers a broken leg when he trips over his untied shoelace on his way back to his delivery vehicle. The claimant owns his delivery vehicle but it is painted with the company logo he is contracted to work with, delivering packages nationally. The claimant is responsible for maintaining the delivery vehicle and is able to work as many or as few hours as he pleases.

Which of the following statements best represents the position in respect of whether the company is vicariously liable for the claimant's injuries?

A. The claimant provides work for the delivery company in return for payment and is likely to be classed as an employee and the company will be vicariously liable for his injuries.

B. As the claimant's vehicle is branded with the company logo, the claimant is likely to be an employee of the company and the company will be vicariously liable for his injuries.

C. On the basis that the claimant has flexible working hours he is likely to be classified as an independent contractor and the company will not be vicariously liable for his injuries.

D. As the company is more likely to have funds available to compensate the claimant, the company will be vicariously liable for the claimant's injuries.

E. The company is unlikely to be vicariously liable for the claimant's injuries as there is no tort committed by the company.

QUESTION 3

The claimant is an experienced steel worker who works at height erecting steel for buildings. His employer fails to provide the claimant with a safety harness and as a result when the claimant loses his footing he falls to his death. The claimant would not have worn the safety harness even if provided with one.

Which of the following statements best represents the position of the court when considering the employer's common law liability for the claimant's death?

A. If the court accepts that the claimant would not have worn a safety harness even if provided with one, the employer will not be liable at common law for the claimant's death.

B. If the court accepts that the claimant would not have worn a safety harness even if provided with one, the employer will be liable at common law for the claimant's death.

C. If the court accepts that the claimant would not have worn a safety harness even if provided with one, the employer will still be liable at common law but the damages awarded will be reduced to reflect contributory negligence on the part of the claimant.

D. If the court finds that the accident could have been prevented by the use of a safety harness, the employer will be liable at common law for the claimant's death.

E. If the court finds that the accident was due to lack of safety equipment, the employer will be liable at common law for the claimant's death.

QUESTION 4

The claimant suffers a serious injury during the course of his employment with the defendant when machinery he is cleaning cuts through the glove he is wearing and causes longstanding nerve damage to his hand. The defendant provides personal protective equipment to all of its employees including gloves, overalls, boots and safety goggles.

Which of the following statements best represents the position of the court in respect of a claim brought against the employer under the common law?

A. The court is likely to find the claimant contributory negligent for placing his hand under the machinery and allowing the machinery to cut through the gloves provided by the defendant.

B. The court is likely to find that the defendant has complied with their common law duty of care in providing a safe system of work and the claimant's claim for damages for breach of duty will fail.

C. The court is likely to find the defendant liable if the claimant can prove what alternative system of work should have been adopted to prevent the accident.

D. The court is likely to find that the defendant has complied with their common law duty of care in providing safe premises and the claimant's claim for damages for breach of duty will fail.

E. The court is likely to find that the defendant has permitted an unsafe practice if the claimant is able to injure his hand whilst wearing gloves which have not protected him, and his claim is likely to succeed.

QUESTION 5

The claimant suffers a serious injury when a work colleague (who is on his first day in the job) fails to place a safety guard on the machinery being used by the claimant. The claimant has to use the emergency 'stop' lever, shutting down the machinery, but not before the equipment has smashed into his shoulder, causing a fractured bone. The new employee had not received any training on the machinery as the trainer responsible was unavailable and the foreman asked the new employee to help them with the work as they had a big order they needed to process.

Which of the following statements best represents the position of the court in respect of a claim brought against the employer under the common law?

A. The court is likely to find that this was a non-fault accident as the employer has provided a training regime and cannot be held liable if the trainer is unavailable due to illness.

B. The court is likely to find that the defendant has failed to comply with their common law duty of care in providing competent staff.

C. The claim is likely to fail on the basis that the defendant has provided competent staff, the claimant should have notified the foreman that the new member of staff was not capable of operating the machinery.

D. The court is likely to find that the defendant has complied with their common law duty of care in providing a safe system of work and the claimant's claim for damages for breach of duty will fail.

E. The court is likely to find the claimant contributory negligent for allowing the new member of staff to assist when he had no formal training on the machinery being used.

■ ANSWERS TO QUESTIONS

Answers to 'What do you know already?' questions at the start of the chapter

1) False – this is one of the two requirements, the other being that the negligent act must have been committed in the course of that person's employment.

2) The economic reality test is used to determine whether an individual is an employee. The test involves three conditions that have to be fulfilled for a worker to be considered an employee. The first that the employee, in return for a wage, provides work or skill for the employer, the second that the employee agrees (expressly or impliedly) that they will work under the control of the employer and the third that the other provisions of the contract are consistent with it being a contract of employment.

3) Complete the missing words. Employers are under a duty to take reasonable care of their employees and liability will arise when employees are injured by a failure to take such care as per the common law principles. The common law principles relate to competent staff, adequate plant and equipment, safe system of work and safe premises.

4) False – an employer will not be held vicariously liable for the negligent acts of an independent contractor.

Answers to end-of-chapter SQE1-style questions

Question 1:
  The answer was D. This is because the court is likely to find that the prison is vicariously liable for the prisoner's negligence as the prisoner is working as an integral part of the operation of the prison. The prisoner and prison have a relationship similar to employer and employee even though the prisoner's presence is not voluntary.

  A is wrong because the prisoner and the prison have a relationship similar to employee/employer.

  B is wrong because what the prisoner is doing is integral to the operation of the prison.

C is wrong because there is an element of control between the prison and the prisoner.

E is wrong because a reduction in damages for contributory negligence reflects the fact that the claimant has contributed to their injuries and this is not the case here.

Question 2:

The answer was E. This is because one party can only be vicariously liable for another party's tort if a tort has been committed. The claimant tripped over his own shoelaces – there is no negligent act and no one is at fault other than the claimant himself.

A, B and C are wrong because a tort has not been committed, but in any event the claimant is likely to be classed as an independent contractor due to the flexibility with which he works.

D is wrong because a tort has not been committed, but having funds available to compensate victims of torts/negligent acts is not a prerequisite for a finding of liability against an employer.

Question 3:

The answer was A. This is based on a real case where the court accepted that the claimant would have refused to wear a safety harness even if the employer had provided one. The defective equipment (or lack of it) did not cause the claimant's accident. Here the claimant's attitude to safety caused the injury.

B is wrong because if the court accept the claimant would not wear safety equipment even if provided they will conclude that the lack of safety equipment is not causative of the injury.

C is wrong because contributory negligence is a defence which reduces damages if the defendant is found to be liable and the claimant is found to have contributed to their injuries. The defendant would not be liable where the claimant's failure to wear safety equipment is the cause of the accident and therefore the defence of contributory negligence would not be considered by the court.

D is wrong because the claimant would not have worn the safety harness even if provided.

E is wrong because the lack of safety equipment did not cause the claimant's injuries, the failure of the claimant to wear safety equipment even if provided caused the claimant's injuries.

Question 4:

The answer was E. This is because the defendant has to provide a safe system of work and adequate equipment. A system which requires an employee to manually clean dangerous machinery is unlikely to be safe. Providing gloves which can be damaged, allowing an employee's hand to be injured, will not be classed as adequate equipment for the purposes of the common law duty.

A is wrong because the claimant's job is to clean the machinery and he should be provided with adequate equipment allowing him to do so without being injured.

B is wrong because allowing employees to manually clean machinery such that the claimant is injured by the machinery is unlikely to be a safe system of work.

C is wrong because it is not for the claimant to prove which alternative system of work would be safer – it is for the employer to provide a safe system of work.

D is wrong because the claim relates to system of work and adequate equipment, not premises.

Question 5:

The answer was B. This is because the employer has a common law duty of care to provide competent staff. Sending staff onto the factory floor without any training is a breach of that common law duty of care.

A is wrong because the employer has a common law duty of care to provide competent staff, which entails training staff to ensure they can do the job.

C is wrong because it is not the responsibility of the claimant to notify his employer about the new member of staff. The employer has a duty of care to provide competent staff.

D is wrong because although the system of work may be safe, allowing an untrained new member of staff is a breach of the employer's duty to provide competent staff and the court will find for the claimant.

E is wrong because the claimant is an employee and it is the employer that has a duty of care to provide safe systems and competent staff. It is not the responsibility of the employee.

■ KEY CASES, RULES, STATUTES AND INSTRUMENTS

The SQE1 Assessment Specification does not require you to recall or recite the cases and statutes referenced in this chapter but does require you to know and understand the principles developed within the cases.

6

Occupiers' liability

■ MAKE SURE YOU KNOW

This chapter will cover principles of occupiers' liability including the legal requirements for a claim under the Occupiers' Liability Act 1957 (in relation to visitors) and the Occupiers' Liability Act 1984 (in relation to non-visitors), defences and exclusion of liability. You are required to know the legal requirements for a claim under the Occupiers' Liability Act 1957 (OLA 1957) and Occupiers' Liability Act 1984 (OLA 1984) and apply the legal principles and rules appropriately and effectively to realistic client-based ethical problems and situations for your SQE1 assessment.

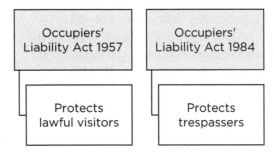

Occupiers' liability

■ SQE ASSESSMENT ADVICE

As you work through this chapter, remember to pay particular attention in your revision to:
• the legal requirements for claims involving visitors to premises
• the legal requirements for claims involving trespassers to premises
• the defences available to occupiers for claims brought by visitors and trespassers

• the situations where liability for harm to visitors/trespassers can be excluded.

■ WHAT DO YOU KNOW ALREADY?

Have a go at these questions before reading this chapter. If you find some difficult or cannot remember the answers, make a note to look more closely at that during your revision.

1) Fill in the blanks.

   Section 1(1) of the Occupiers' Liability Act 1957 regulates the duty which an _____ owes to his _____ in respect of dangers due to the state of the _____ or to things done or omitted to be done on them.

   [Occupiers' Liability Act 1957, pages 115–121]

2) What is not covered under the OLA 1984?

   a) liability for trespasser's personal injury

   b) liability for trespasser's damage to property

   c) liability for trespasser's death.

   [Occupiers' Liability Act 1984, pages 121–124]

3) What defences are available for claims brought under the OLA (1957 and 1984)?

   [Occupiers' Liability Act 1957, pages 124–125]

4) What are the special categories of visitors under the OLA 1957 where the court applies a different standard of care?

   [Occupiers' Liability Act 1957, pages 117–119]

OCCUPIERS' LIABILITY

Two pieces of legislation protect those injured by the state of other's premises – the Occupiers' Liability Act 1957 (OLA 1957), which seeks to protect lawful **visitors** from injury, and the Occupiers' Liability Act 1984, which protects all others (**trespassers**) from injury.

Key term: visitor

A lawful visitor to premises is one that has a right to enter (eg, police), or one that is invited (eg, a hotel guest) or one whose presence has not been objected to (eg, postal delivery person delivering mail).

> **Key term: trespasser**
>
> A trespasser is one who goes onto land without any invitation and whose presence may be unknown to the occupier, or if known, is objected to.

OCCUPIERS' LIABILITY ACT 1957

Under section 1(1) of the OLA 1957, the Act regulates 'the duty which an **occupier** of premises owes to his visitors in respect of dangers due to the state of the premises or to things done or omitted to be done on them'. The SQE1 Assessment Specification requires that you know the legal requirements for a claim under the Occupiers' Liability Act 1957 (in relation to visitors). **Table 6.1** illustrates how the court has defined the terms within the Act.

> **Key term: occupier**
>
> An occupier is one with a legal right to control the premises.

Table 6.1: Key terms and example cases (OLA 1957)

Key term	Examples
Occupier	Normally the occupier will have an element of control over the premises (s1(2)) and for this reason there may be more than one occupier. In *Wheat v E. Lacon & Co Ltd [1966] AC 552 (HL)* the brewery and the managers to whom they had let their public house were both deemed to be occupiers under the OLA 1957 when a guest staying at the pub died after falling down the stairs.
Control	Control can also refer to a legal right to control the premises, even if the defendant does not take physical possession of the premises. In *Harris v Birkenhead Corporation [1976] 1 WLR 279 (CA)* the council were held to be occupiers' of derelict property after they took control of the property but did not secure it and a young child wandered in and was injured when she fell through a vandalised window.

Key terms and example cases (OLA 1957) (continued)

Key term	Examples
Premises	The definition is wide and includes 'any fixed or moveable structure, including any vessel, vehicle or aircraft' (s1(3)(a)). In *Jolley v Sutton London Borough Council* [2000] 1 WLR 1082 (HL) the court found an abandoned boat on council ground to be premises.
Visitor	Lawful visitors include the following: a) those with express permission, for example friends that you invite to your house b) those with implied permission, for example a delivery driver dropping off a parcel c) those under contract, for example workmen carrying out work under a contract for service d) those with a right to enter, for example the police. The court has recognised situations where a claimant has started as a visitor and due to their behaviour or the restriction by the occupier they have ceased to be a visitor and would fall outside the Act. For example, a customer in a supermarket is a visitor; they have implied permission to enter and shop. However, should they stray into the loading bay through a door with a sign prohibiting the public and displaying a 'staff only' sign they would no longer be a visitor for the purposes of OLA 1957 and would become a trespasser.

Exam warning

Remember, an occupier may not necessarily be the owner of the land. The occupier will have an element of control over the premises, may not even be in situ on the premises and may have joint responsibility with another.

We have considered the definitions of the terms under the OLA 1957 and we now turn to the duty of care expected under the Act.

Duty of care under OLA 1957

Section 2(2) states the duty of care. It is 'to take such care as in all the circumstances of the case is reasonable to see that the visitor will be reasonably safe in using the premises for the purposes for which he is invited or permitted by the occupier to be there.' We have already considered the standard of care in respect of negligence in **Chapter 1** and the standard is similar under the OLA 1957. Where visitors are vulnerable and the occupier has full knowledge of the vulnerability, the court will expect the occupier to take steps to guard against it. For example, an open window on a second-floor property would not fail to make a visitor reasonably safe; however, the occupier would be in breach of the Act if a blind person was visiting and fell out of the window, suffering injury (*Pollock v Cahill* [2015] EWHC 2260 (QB)).

The type of damage covered under OLA 1957 is personal injury (including death) and property damage.

Revision tip

When revising an occupier's duty of care under OLA 1957, think about the basic principles of negligence the court will take into account, namely, what is reasonable in all the circumstances. Consider what is the likelihood of harm, the nature of the danger, the type of visitor and their purpose of visiting, the seriousness and longevity of the risk, the cost of prevention and whether there were any warning signs.

Exam warning

Remember, duty of care dictates that a visitor is reasonably safe on the premises, not that the premises are safe. It is a common mistake to assume this means that the duty is to ensure that the premises are safe. If a warning sign is displayed or an area cordoned off advising visitors of the dangers of a certain part of the occupiers' premises, the duty will be complied with.

Special categories

The OLA 1957 allows for a deviation from the usual standard of care in respect of children and skilled workers. **Figure 6.1** illustrates how the duty differs.

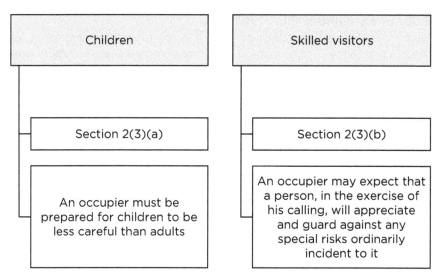

Figure 6.1: Duty of care: special categories

Table 6.2 illustrates how the court deals with the duty of care for special categories under the OLA 1957. These will be familiar as we have considered the standard of care and special categories in respect of negligence in **Chapter 1**.

Table 6.2: Duty of care: special categories OLA 1957

Special duty of care	Example case
Children The court will take into account the age of the child and the risk posed.	A 15-year-old boy was hit by a train whilst walking on the railway line. The court held no duty of care was owed due to the fact a 15-year-old should be aware of the dangers associated with the railway. *Titchener v BRB* [1983] 1 WLR 1427 (HL) A two-year-old drowned in a pond at a holiday park. A small fence surrounding the pool did not prevent the boy from entering the pond. The court found that the danger of a pond to a small child if the child wandered off was obvious (to parents) and that it was not necessary for the occupier to emphasise that danger. The occupier was not liable. *Bourne Leisure v Marsdon* [2009] EWCA Civ 671

Duty of care: special categories OLA 1957 (continued)

Special duty of care	Example case
	A five-year-old playing on a building site being developed by the council fell down a trench. The court held the occupier could assume the parents having responsibility for their children would not allow them to play on a building site. The occupier was not liable.
	Phipps v Rochester Corporation [1955] 1 QB 450 (DC)
If there is a danger of allurement on the land the occupier will be expected to take greater care.	A 14-year-old was injured when an abandoned boat (on council owned land) he and his friends had been working on fell on him. The boat, which had been in situ for two years, posed an allurement to children and the council was liable to the claimant.
	Jolley v Sutton London Borough Council [2000] 1 WLR 1082 (HL)
Skilled workers

The occupier still has a duty towards skilled workers but the court will look at the nature of the risk.

Skilled workers are expected to take extra care to guard against risks associated with their profession. | Two chimney sweeps attending a property to work on the chimney flues were warned about the risks of working on flues where vents were sealed but continued to do so and died due to carbon monoxide poisoning.

The court held that as specialists they were expected to know and guard against the risks of such danger.

Roles v Nathan [1963] 1 WLR 1117 (CA) |

Exam warning

If asked about the duty of care owed to a skilled worker exercising his calling, think about the type of risk and whether it is an obvious risk the skilled worker should have been aware of. For example, an electrician injured due to failing to switch the electric off at the mains and working on wiring would not be successful in claiming against an occupier as knowledge of the risks of electricity are integral to the electrician's work.

Warnings

Section 2(4)(a) of the OLA 1957 provides some protection for occupiers where claimants have been warned about the danger; however, the warning will not absolve an occupier from liability unless in all the circumstances it was enough to enable the visitor to be reasonably safe. This means that the court will consider the type of danger and the warning given and ascertain whether the warning was enough to keep the visitor reasonably safe.

If the danger is obvious, the occupier need not warn against it and can rely upon the openly apparent risk posed by the danger to alert the claimant to potential danger. For example, in *Darby v National Trust* [2001] EWCA Civ 189 the defendant's failure to place 'no swimming' signs around a pond they knew the public swam in did not find them in breach of section 2 under the OLA 1957 as the court held that the notices would have told the claimant no more than he knew due to the obvious risk posed by swimming in open water.

If the danger is not obvious the occupier will be held liable if they fail to adequately warn visitors. For example, in *English Heritage v Taylor* [2016] EWCA Civ 2760 (QB) the claimant succeeded in a claim under OLA 1957 when he fell over a sheer drop whilst visiting Carlsbrooke Castle. The court found that the drop was not obvious and the defendant occupier should have placed a sign warning of the drop.

Figure 6.2 illustrates factors which should be considered when dealing with warning signs and the risk posed.

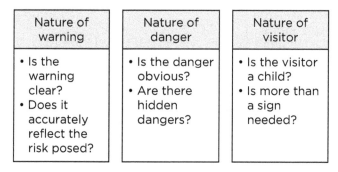

Nature of warning	Nature of danger	Nature of visitor
• Is the warning clear? • Does it accurately reflect the risk posed?	• Is the danger obvious? • Are there hidden dangers?	• Is the visitor a child? • Is more than a sign needed?

Figure 6.2: Warnings OLA 1957

Independent contractors

Where an occupier employs an independent contractor to undertake work, and a visitor is injured due to the faulty execution of that work, the occupier will not be liable if they have discharged their duty of care. The three requirements under the OLA 1957 are that the occupier must have:

a) entrusted the work to a competent contractor
b) taken reasonable steps to ensure the contractor was competent
c) taken reasonable care to ensure the work was properly done.

Section 2(4)(b) of the OLA 1957 stipulates that the work must be work of 'construction, maintenance or repair'. The more technical and complex the work, the more likely the duty of care will be discharged by engaging a reputable contractor. In *Haseldine v Daw & Son Ltd* [1941] 2 KB 343 (CA) the occupier entrusted the maintenance of lifts at his block of flats to an engineering firm and when the lift failed and injured a tenant the court held that the technicalities of servicing a lift was not work that the occupier could reasonably be expected to check. In contrast where the nature of the work is not complex the court will expect an occupier to notice when the work is defective. In *Woodward v Mayor of Hastings* [1945] KB 174 (CA), the occupier was held liable for failing to check that the cleaner tasked with removing ice from the steps at a school had done so properly, on the basis that clearing ice was straightforward.

OCCUPIERS' LIABILITY ACT 1984

Under the OLA 1957 a common duty of care is owed to 'visitors'. The Occupiers' Liability Act 1984 (OLA 1984) relates to 'non-visitors' (trespassers) who have neither the occupiers' express nor implied permission to be on the premises. The Act also applies to people exercising a right of way and visitors to land covered by the National Parks and Access to the Countryside Act 1949. Like the OLA 1957, the definitions of 'occupier' and 'premises' are the same. Damage to property is not covered under the OLA 1984, only personal injury.

Duty of care under OLA 1984

A duty of care does not arise automatically under OLA 1984; Section 1(3) outlines the three conditions which must be satisfied:

a) The occupier is aware of the danger or has reasonable grounds to believe it exists.
b) The occupier knows or has reasonable grounds to believe that the trespasser is in the vicinity of the danger.
c) The risk is one against which in all the circumstances the occupier may reasonably be expected to offer some protection.

The risk of injury must be due to the state of the premises. **Practice example 6.1** illustrates how the courts have dealt with this point.

Practice example 6.1

The claimant was seriously injured when he attempted a shallow dive in a lake managed by the defendant. Signs around the lake prohibited swimming. The defendant knew people swam in the lake and had intended to plant vegetation to prevent access but due to financial restraints had not done so at the time of the accident. Had the defendants breached their duty of care?

This is what the court had to consider in *Tomlinson v Congleton Borough Council* [2004] 1 AC 46. The court found that the risk arose due to what the claimant did on the premises, not because of the state of the premises. When the claimant ignored the signs prohibiting swimming, he became a trespasser as he exceeded his implied permission as a visitor in the park as he entered the water. The court held that although the defendant was aware of the danger and had reasonable grounds to believe trespassers in the vicinity swam in the lake, the risk was one which the defendant could not be reasonably expected to offer protection against. The court found that diving into the lake involved obvious risks that the defendant should not be expected to guard against.

Table 6.3 considers each element of the duty of care.

Table 6.3: S1(3) OLA 1984 conditions

Condition	Example case
The occupier is aware of the danger or has reasonable grounds to believe it exists.	The occupier has to know about the danger: Diving into a lake, ignoring signs stating 'private property, strictly no swimming allowed', the claimant hit his head on a hidden fibreglass container, the existence of which the defendant had no knowledge. The court held that, as the occupier did not know, nor had reasonable grounds to believe the container existed, there was no liability on the occupier. *Rhind v Astbury Water Park Ltd* [2004] EWCA Civ 756

S1(3) OLA 1984 conditions (continued)

Condition	Example case
The occupier knows or has reasonable grounds to believe that the trespasser is in the vicinity of the danger.	The occupier has to be aware of the existence of previous non-visitors: Climbing through a gap in a high fence and climbing onto a factory roof, the nine-year-old claimant fell through a skylight. The court held that the occupier did not know (nor had grounds to believe) children were in the vicinity and the claim failed. *Swain v Puri* [1996] PIQR P442 (CA) Also, the occupier must know that the non-visitors are 'in the vicinity' of the danger: The occupier had knowledge that trespassers swam in the harbour in the summer but had no reason to believe they would do so in the winter and the claim failed. *Donoghue v Folkestone Properties Ltd* [2003] EWCA Civ 231
The risk is one against which, in all the circumstances, the occupier may reasonably be expected to offer some protection.	The court will not impose a duty where it is unreasonable to do so: A five-year-old injured on a swing on a playground near to a school field being used for sports day was owed no duty of care as playing fields could not be made hazard free and it was unreasonable to expect the school to fence off the playground. *Simonds v Isle of Wight Council* [2003] EWHC 2303 (QB)

The duty of care under OLA 1984 is not as onerous as under the OLA 1957 as the occupier only needs to take 'such care as is reasonable in all the circumstances'; this includes factors such as:
• the type of risk involved – was the risk obvious or a hidden risk?
• the type of trespasser – children? vulnerable adults?
• whether the risk could have been reduced.

The court also takes into account the fact that the trespasser has not been invited onto the premises. Outcomes could be quite different if the claimant was a visitor as opposed to a trespasser. Consider how the case of *Rhind*, outlined in Table 6.3, would have been different if the claim proceeded under the OLA 1957; the court would likely find that the occupier *should* have known about the container in the lake if 'visitors' were swimming there and the occupier would have breached the duty of care under the OLA 1957.

DEFENCES

There is no specific distinction between the defences under both OLA 1957 and OLA 1984. The defences will be familiar from **Chapter 4**. **Table 6.4** compares the defences available under the Acts.

Table 6.4: Defences under the Occupiers' Liability Acts

Defence	OLA 1957	OLA 1984
Volenti (consent)	The defence applies if the visitor knew, understood and accepted the precise risk.	The defence of consent is not specifically mentioned in the Act but it will apply in the same manner as it would for the 1957 Act; ie, if the visitor knew, understood and accepted the precise risk the defendant would have a defence.
Restrict/modify/exclude duty	An occupier can restrict, extend, modify or exclude their liability. The exclusion notice must be brought to the claimant's attention and the wording of the notice must cover the loss suffered.	Again, this is not specifically referred to in the 1984 Act but a defendant could use similar principles as the 1957 Act to restrict, modify or exclude liability.
Warnings	The warning must enable the visitor in 'all the circumstances' to be safe.	The occupier may discharge their duty to trespassers by giving warnings to discourage entry to trespassers. The occupier only needs to take 'reasonable steps' to alert the claimant to danger.

Defences under the Occupiers' Liability Acts (continued)

Defence	OLA 1957	OLA 1984
Contributory negligence	The Law Reform (Contributory Negligence) Act 1945 applies and the court will reduce damages to the extent they find the claimant contributed to their injuries.	The same statutory legislation applies to trespassers.

Exclusion of liability

An occupier may seek to exclude or limit their liability under the OLA 1957 by setting out a notice which allows the visitor to understand the conditions upon which the visitor is entering the occupier's premises. The notice must be brought to the visitor's attention. By setting out the conditions to the visitor the occupier can attempt to prevent a duty of care arising. For example, a sign on clear display before entry to a car park stating 'Vehicles are left in the car park at the owner's risk. The management accept no responsibility for loss or damage caused to any vehicles or its contents.' Liability for damage to property can be excluded as long as it fulfils the conditions referred to in Table 6.4. However occupiers cannot exclude liability for death or personal injury. A notice in a car park stating 'The management accept no responsibility for death or personal injury howsoever caused on their premises' would be deemed in breach of the Unfair Contract Terms Act 1977 which prevents exclusion of liability for death and personal injury. There is no such provision applicable to private premises, so an occupier of private premises could provide a notice restricting, excluding or limiting their liability.

Revision tip

You are required to know for SQE1 purposes that occupiers cannot exclude liability for death or personal injury. It is useful to understand the different Acts providing protection against exclusion of liability. One for business-to-business relationships and the other for business-to-consumer relationships. Therefore if the occupier is a trader or business the Unfair Contract Terms Act 1977 (UCTA 1977) prevents exclusion of liability for death and personal injury. If the occupier is a trader or business and the visitor a consumer, the Consumer Rights Act 2015 (CRA 2015) prevents exclusion of liability for death and personal injury and protects consumers.

Unlike the OLA 1957, the OLA 1984 makes no reference to whether an occupier can exclude liability in respect of trespassers. A trespasser would not be a consumer for the purposes of CRA 2015 nor would they be a business or trader for the purposes of UCTA 1977, therefore neither of these Acts would apply.

Compensation Act 2006

The Compensation Act allows the court to consider whether imposing a duty of care would prevent or discourage people from undertaking desirable activity. This could be volunteers organising charity or sports events and provides reassurance to those involved that failure to take precautions will not lead to a finding of liability if taking those precautions would have prevented the activity from going ahead. Section 2 also provides that an apology or the taking of steps to remedy a situation should not amount to an admission of liability. The Act has been viewed as an attempt to stem what some have termed a 'compensation culture' and allow organisers of public events freedom to engage with the public without fear of claims.

■ KEY POINT CHECKLIST

This chapter has covered the following key knowledge points. You can use these to structure your revision around, making sure to recall the key details for each point, as covered in this chapter.

- Under the OLA 1957 an occupier owes a duty of care to lawful visitors on their premises in respect of dangers due to the state of the premises.
- An occupier under the OLA 1957 is a person with an element of physical control over the premises but does not need to be the owner of the land.
- Premises under the OLA 1957 includes any fixed or moveable structure.
- A lawful visitor under the OLA 1957 includes those with express or implied permission and those with a right of entry.
- Occupiers need to take greater care where children are involved and the court will take into consideration the child's age and whether there is a dangerous allurement against which the occupier should take greater care.
- Skilled workers are expected to take extra care and the court will look at the nature of the risk.
- Warnings may offer a defendant some protection under the OLA 1957 and the court will consider the type of danger and the nature of the warning given.

- Where a visitor is injured due to the work of an independent contractor the occupier will not be liable under the OLA 1957 as long as the occupier was reasonable in entrusting the work to the independent contractor and took reasonable steps to ensure the independent contractor was competent and took reasonable care to ensure that the work was properly done.
- An occupier will be liable under the OLA 1984 for the personal injury (not damage to property) of a trespasser injured due to the state of premises if the occupier is aware of the danger or has reasonable grounds to believe it exists and the occupier knows or has reasonable grounds to believe that the trespasser is in the vicinity of the danger and the risk is one against which in all the circumstances the occupier may reasonably be expected to offer some protection.
- In respect of claims brought under the OLA 1984 the court will take into consideration the type of risk involved, the type of trespasser and whether the risk could have been reduced.
- An occupier may successfully defend a claim brought under the OLA 1957 and OLA 1984 if there were warning signs alerting visitors/ trespassers to the danger, if the visitor/trespasser consented to the risk or if the visitor/trespasser contributed to the injury sustained. An occupier may also exclude, restrict or modify liability under the Acts.
- Occupiers are unable to exclude liability for death and personal injury under OLA 1957.

■ KEY TERMS AND CONCEPTS

- visitor (**page 114**)
- trespasser (**page 115**)
- occupier (**page 115**)

■ SQE1-STYLE QUESTIONS

QUESTION 1

The claimant visits the defendant's pub. The pub is on two floors and has a grand open staircase with bannisters on either side leading down to the ground floor. As she is leaving the pub, the claimant attempts to slide down the bannister of the staircase and falls, seriously injuring herself. There are no warning signs alerting customers to the dangers of the bannister or the 4 metre drop either side of them.

Which of the following is likely to be the position of the court when considering the defendant's argument that the claimant accepted the risk of injury?

A. The court is likely to find there is no liability for risks accepted by the claimant and that in sliding down the bannister the claimant accepted the risk of injuring herself.

B. The court is likely to find liability attaches to the defendant as although the claimant may have accepted the risk, had the defendant erected warning signs, the claimant would not have attempted to slide down the bannister.

C. The court is likely to find there is no liability under either the Occupiers' Liability Act 1957 or 1984 as the claimant was neither a visitor nor a trespasser when she slid down the bannister.

D. The court is likely to find that liability attaches to the defendant as it was foreseeable that an old building with architectural attractive features would act as an allurement for those that have consumed alcohol.

E. The court is likely to find the defendant liable under the Occupiers' Liability Act 1957 but reduce the claimant's damages to reflect contributory negligence on her part.

QUESTION 2

The claimant is a seven-year-old boy who wanders through a council-owned public park with his friends and picks and eats berries from shrubbery around the park. The berries are poisonous and the boy dies.

Which of the following is likely to be the court's approach to the defendant's argument in their defence to the claim that being poisoned by eating berries is an obvious risk and one they do not need to warn visitors about?

A. The court is likely to find that the parents of the claimant should have prevented him from eating the berries and the defendant will not be liable.

B. The court is likely to find the claimant a trespasser and as the defendant took such care as is reasonable in all the circumstances no liability will attach to the defendant.

C. The court is likely to find that a child of seven years would know that berries should not be eaten, and no liability will attach to the defendant.

D. The court is likely to find the council at fault for failing to warn visitors but will reduce the claimant's damages to reflect that the claimant accepted the risk in willingly eating the berries.

E. The court will take into account the age of the child, the risk posed by the poisonous berries and the fact that there were no warning signs to alert the public to the danger and find the defendant liable.

QUESTION 3

The claimant is attending a council-owned gym when the pedals on the equipment he was exercising on suddenly fail, causing him injury when he is thrown from the equipment. The council have employed independent contractors to inspect and maintain all their gym equipment. The independent contractors undertook only a very limited inspection six weeks prior to the claimant's accident which shows no faults on the equipment.

Which of the following is likely to be the position of the court when considering whether the council is liable for the claimant's injury?

A. The court is likely to find that the council is liable as the claimant was a visitor injured by the state of the council's premises.

B. The court is likely to find that the council is not liable as the risk of injury on gym equipment is an obvious one against which the council cannot be expected to protect the gym users.

C. The court is likely to find that the council and the independent contractors are equally liable for the claimant's injuries due to the faulty equipment.

D. The court is likely to find that the council is not liable as they have entrusted the inspection and maintenance of the gym equipment to competent independent contractors.

E. The court is likely to find that the council is liable for the claimant's injuries as the council should not have relied upon the work of the independent contractors.

QUESTION 4

The claimant is visiting a castle at a heritage site when he wanders along a corridor and sees a door with a large sign stating: 'no entry – steep staircase, strictly private – keep out'. Intrigued by what is behind the door, the claimant enters and starts to descend a staircase when he loses his footing and slips from the top to the bottom of the steps. In doing so he breaks his leg and wrist. He also smashes his mobile phone and the expensive camera he was carrying.

Which of the following is likely to be the court's approach to the claimant's claim against the occupier?

A. The court will likely find the occupier liable under the Occupiers' Liability Act 1957 as the claimant was a visitor and they failed to take reasonable care of him.

B. The court will likely find the occupier liable under the Occupiers' Liability Act 1984 as the claimant is a trespasser and the occupier has failed to keep him reasonably safe by locking the door at the end of the corridor.

C. The court will likely accept that the claimant became a trespasser when he walked through the 'no entry' door but find that the occupier has done all that is reasonable to keep the claimant safe by placing a 'no entry' sign on it.

D. The court will likely accept that the claimant was a visitor but that the risk of injury was obvious if not taking care when walking down stairs and the occupier will not be liable.

E. The court will likely find the occupier liable under the Occupiers' Liability Act 1984 and compensate the claimant for his injuries and his damaged phone and camera.

QUESTION 5

The claimant is attending a concert in the city centre and parks her car in the concert's venue car park. The car park is in an area of the city centre that has a high crime rate and there have been many car thefts from the car park, which has been targeted by gangs over the last few months. As she enters the car park the claimant sees many large signs displayed stating: 'The management accept no liability for damage to or loss of property, personal injury or death. Vehicles (and their contents) are parked at the owner's risk. Please remove any items of value from your vehicle and ensure your vehicle is locked before leaving the car park.' The claimant returns to the car park after the concert to find that her car has been broken into and the claimant's laptop stolen from the back seat of her car.

Which of the following is likely to be the court's approach to the claimant's claim against the owner of the car park for the loss of her laptop?

A. The court is likely to find the car park owners liable for the loss of property on the basis that an occupier is unable to exclude liability for property and personal injury.

B. The court is likely to find the car park owners liable for the claimant's loss of property on the basis that an occupier is unable to exclude liability for property damage.

C. The court is unlikely to find the car park owners liable for the claimant's loss of property as the exclusion notice is clearly displayed and has been brought to the claimant's attention and the wording of the notice covers the loss suffered.

D. The court is likely to find the exclusion notice unclear as to whether the occupier would be liable for the loss of property from the back seat of the claimant's car and the claim would fail.

E. The court is likely to find car park owners liable for the loss of the claimant's property as they have failed to take precautions to prevent their customer's property being damaged by criminal gangs in the city centre.

■ ANSWERS TO QUESTIONS

Answers to 'What do you know already?' questions at the start of the chapter

1) Section 1(1) of the Occupiers' Liability Act 1957 regulates the duty which an *occupier of premises* owes to his *visitors* in respect of dangers due to the state of the *premises* or to things done or omitted to be done on them.

2) The answer was (b). Damage to property is not covered under the OLA 1984.

3) The defences available under the Occupiers' Liability Act (1957 and 1984) are consent, reliance on any restriction, modification or exclusion of liability, warnings or contributory negligence.

4) The special categories of visitors that the court will apply a different standard of care to are children and skilled visitors.

Answers to end-of-chapter SQE1-style questions

Question 1:

The correct answer was A. This is because the court is likely to find there is no liability for risks accepted by the claimant and that in sliding down the bannister the claimant accepted the risk of injuring herself. The OLA 1957 provides that the common duty of care does not impose on an occupier any duty for risks which are willingly accepted by the visitor. A warning sign was not required as the risk was obvious (and indeed may have encouraged those that had not thought about sliding down the bannisters to slide down them).

B is wrong because the OLA 1957 does not impose a duty for risks willingly accepted by the visitor. A warning sign was not necessary as the risk was so obvious.

C is wrong because the claimant was a visitor for the purposes of the OLA 1957.

D is wrong because a bannister is not an allurement and the claimant accepted the risk of falling when she decided to slide down the bannister.

E is wrong because the defendant has a complete defence on the basis that the claimant willingly accepted the risk of injuring herself. Contributory negligence only applies as a defence where the defendant has been found liable for the claimant's injuries.

Question 2:

The correct answer was E. This is because the court will take into account the age of the child – a seven-year-old would not be expected to understand the danger posed by the berries – they are bright and potentially an allurement. The risk posed by the poisonous berries in a public park where children play freely is high. The fact that there were no warning signs to alert the public to the danger is detrimental to the defendant. Signs are practical and cheap to install.

A is wrong because it is common for children to wander around parks both with and without parents.

B is wrong because the claimant is a visitor as the park was council owned and for the enjoyment of the public.

C is wrong because a child of seven years is unlikely to appreciate that berries could be poisonous.

D is wrong because a child of seven years would not appreciate nor could they accept the risk of eating the berries.

Question 3:

The correct answer was D. This is because the council are reasonable in entrusting the inspection and maintenance to an independent contractor. The court found that the inspection had been defective as it was limited but that the council were entitled to rely on the independent contractors as they were experts.

A is wrong because, although the claimant is a visitor and is injured by the state of the claimant's premises, the council can defend the claim on the basis that they relied upon the instruction of independent contractors.

B is wrong because the risk of injury is not obvious. Gym users do not expect to be injured by the gym equipment.

C is wrong because the independent contractors will be liable and the council will escape liability.

E is wrong because the council were entitled to entrust the inspection and maintenance to experts.

Question 4:

The correct answer was C. This is because the claimant exceeds his permission as a visitor the minute he enters through the 'no entry' door and becomes a trespasser. The duty under the Act is to take such care as is reasonable in all the circumstances. Also, the injury must be due to the state of the premises. The claimant has lost his footing and there is no suggestion that the stairs are defective. Further, by placing a sign on the door the defendant was ensuring that visitors do not enter places which are not accessible to the public.

A is wrong because the claimant becomes a trespasser the instant he exceeds his permission and walks through the 'no entry' door. The OLA 1984 is the relevant Act not the OLA 1957.

B is wrong because, although the claimant is a trespasser and the relevant act is the OLA 1984, the court is unlikely to find it reasonable to lock a door through which staff need to enter. There is no 'danger' to warn the claimant about, he has simply lost his footing on the stairs.

D is wrong because the claimant becomes a trespasser the instant he walks through the 'no entry' door.

E is wrong because the claimant is at fault for his injury by losing his footing but in any event property damage cannot be claimed under OLA 1984.

Question 5:

The correct answer was C. This is because the exclusion notice is clearly displayed and has been brought to the claimant's attention, as the question states that the claimant has seen the sign as she enters. Also, the exclusion notice covers the loss as it mentions property within the vehicles.

A is wrong because an occupier can exclude liability for property damage as long as the exclusion notice is clearly displayed and has been brought to the claimant's attention and the wording of the notice covers the loss suffered, but an occupier cannot exclude liability for personal injury or death.

B is wrong because an occupier can exclude liability for property damage.

D is wrong because the exclusion notice is clear and the wording relates to the loss suffered, namely property stolen from vehicles.

E is wrong because occupiers are able to exclude liability under OLA 1957 as long as the exclusion notice is clearly displayed and has been brought to the claimant's attention and the wording of the notice covers the loss suffered. An increase in the crime rate in the area has no bearing on whether the court will find the exclusion notice reasonable.

■ KEY CASES, RULES, STATUTES AND INSTRUMENTS

The SQE1 Assessment Specification requires you to know the following key statutes:

• Occupiers' Liability Act 1957
• Occupiers' Liability Act 1984

You should also be familiar with the following statutes after this chapter but you do not need to recall or recite them for the purposes of SQE1:

• Law Reform (Contributory Negligence) Act 1945
• Compensation Act 2006
• Unfair Contract Terms Act 1977
• Consumer Rights Act 2015

7

Product liability

■ MAKE SURE YOU KNOW

Previous chapters concentrated on the requirements in establishing negligence in respect of injury and death. This chapter concentrates on liability for defective products. You are required to know the principles in common law negligence and the Consumer Protection Act 1987 in respect of product liability and apply the legal principles and rules appropriately and effectively to realistic client-based ethical problems and situations for your SQE1 assessment. The topic areas are shown here.

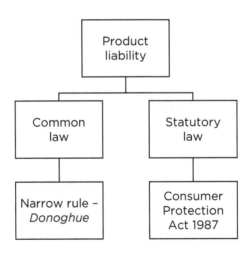

Product liability

■ SQE ASSESSMENT ADVICE

As you work through this chapter, remember to pay particular attention in your revision to:
- when a claim for product liability can arise
- the requirements under the common law
- the requirements under the Consumer Protection Act 1987 (CPA 1987)
- defences available to claims brought in respect of product liability.

■ WHAT DO YOU KNOW ALREADY?

Have a go at these questions before reading this chapter. If you find some difficult or cannot remember the answers, make a note to look more closely at that during your revision.

1) What is the common law duty between manufacturer and consumer?

   [Common law, pages 137–139]

2) What are the defences available to a manufacturer faced with a claim under the common law?

   [Defences, pages 139–140]

3) Which of the following are classified as manufacturers for the purpose of the common law?

   a) suppliers

   b) repairers

   c) retailers

   d) distributors

   [Manufacturers, page 142]

4) True or false?

   Anyone supplying defective products is strictly liable in tort under s 2(1) Consumer Protection Act 1987.

   [Consumer Protection Act 1987, pages 140–143]

5) Is it possible to exclude liability under the Consumer Protection Act 1987?

   [Consumer Protection Act 1987, pages 140–143]

PRODUCT LIABILITY

Liability for defective products can arise under several areas of law including contract law and consumer law. This chapter will concentrate on tortious liability arising out of the common law and under the Consumer Protection Act (CPA) 1987.

COMMON LAW

The common law position on product liability originates from the case of *Donoghue v Stevenson* [1932] AC 562 (HL) (see **Chapter 1**). Although you are not required to know the details of this case for the purpose of the SQE1, it is worth being familiar with it. The case developed the 'neighbour principle' which ensures that you must take reasonable care to avoid acts and omissions which you can reasonably foresee would be likely to injure your neighbour. This is sometimes referred to as the 'wide rule'.

As the case involved a defective product, the judgement also gave guidance on the relationship between manufacturer and ultimate consumer. This is known as the 'narrow rule'. In order to establish a duty of care between manufacturer and ultimate consumer, several elements must be present. **Figure 7.1** outlines these elements and **Table 7.1** defines them in more detail.

Manufacturer	Products	Ultimate consumer	Intermediate examination
• The defendant must be the manufacturer	• The product must have caused damage	• Anyone foreseeably affected by the product	• Manufacturer believed it likely product would be examined by an intermediate – no liability

Figure 7.1: 'Narrow rule' elements

Table 7.1: Narrow rule defined

Element of the narrow rule	Explanation
Manufacturer	Widely defined by the courts as anyone who has worked on the product before it reaches the consumer and includes suppliers, assemblers, retailers, installers and repairers of products.
	In *Andrews v Hopkinson* [1957] 1 QB 229 (QBD) a car dealer (supplier) of a car with defective steering was held liable as the defect could have been noted on inspection by a mechanic and due to the seriousness of the consequence of supplying a car with defective steering.

Narrow rule defined (continued)

Element of the narrow rule	Explanation
Product	Widely defined as anything capable of causing damage. Includes anything that accompanies the product, for example, packing, tags, labels, instructions. In *Vacwell Engineering Co Ltd v BDH Chemicals Ltd* [1971] 1 QB 111 (CA) the liable defendant failed to include safety instructions to warn about the potential hazards of allowing its chemical product to come into contact with water.
Ultimate consumer	Widely defined as anyone who it would be reasonably foreseeable to be affected by the product (the neighbour principle). If the claimant knew about the dangerous product but continues to use it the defendant will not be liable. In *Howmet Ltd v Economy Devices Ltd* [2016] EWCA Civ 847 manufacturers of a (defective) product used to avert the risk of fire were not liable when the claimant's factory burnt down as the claimant was aware the device was malfunctioning.
Intermediate examination	If prior to the product being supplied to the ultimate consumer an intermediate is reasonably expected to examine the product (thus revealing the defect), the chain of causation will be broken and the manufacturer will not be liable. The intermediate could be liable if they failed to examine and spot the defect. In *Kubach v Hollands* [1937] 3 All ER 907 (KBD) a schoolgirl was injured whilst using chemicals purchased by her teacher from the second defendants (the intermediates) who in turn had purchased them from a third party. The third party's invoice to the second defendants stipulated that the chemicals needed to be examined and tested before use. The second defendants were held liable for failing to examine the product before selling it to the school.

Exam warning

If the only loss incurred by the claimant is the defective product, or the cost of repairing or replacing the product, then this amounts to economic loss (see **Chapter 3**) and this is not recoverable in negligence.

Revision tip

Remember that the standard of care is that which is reasonable and questions of product liability at common law mean that the manufacturer will be judged by the standards of a 'reasonable' manufacturer.

As product liability at common law is based on the narrow rule in *Donoghue*, in order to successfully bring a claim for injury caused by a defective product the claimant needs to prove breach of duty, causation and damage, the same as for any negligence claim (see **Chapter 1**). The claimant has to prove that 'but for' the defendant's negligence the claimant would not have suffered the injury. **Practice example 7.1** illustrates how these common law principles are reflected in product liability claims.

Practice example 7.1

The claimant buys a car fitted with a toughened safety glass windscreen. After about a year the windscreen smashes, causing injury from fragments of glass. Are the manufacturers of the glass responsible for the defective glass?

This is what the court had to consider in *Evans v Triplex Safety Glass Co Ltd* [1936] 1 All ER 283. The court found that the lapse of time between the purchase of the car and the incident occurring was too long. The court also referenced that the glass could have been strained when screwed into its frame, there was potentially an opportunity for examination by the intermediate seller and that the breaking of the glass might have been caused by something other than a defect in manufacture.

Defences
Defences were discussed in detail in **Chapter 4**. By way of recap, there are three potential defences in common law. They are:
• consent
• contributory negligence
• exclusion of liability.

Consent
If the claimant is aware of the defect and continues to use the product the manufacturer may be able to defend the claim. The defendant

must show that the claimant knew of the risk, accepted it willingly and continued to use the product.

Contributory negligence

The defendant may be able to partially defend a claim on the basis that the claimant contributed to their injuries. For example if a claimant realised the product was not performing as it should but continued to use it and was injured in the process the defendant may argue that the claimant was aware of the defect and contributed to his own injuries.

Exclusion of liability

We have seen that in the course of business/trade liability in negligence for personal injury and death cannot be excluded (**Chapter 6**) under the Unfair Contract Terms Act 1977 (UCTA) and the Consumer Rights Act 2015 (CRA). However, in respect of other loss (such as damage or injury caused by product liability), liability can be excluded (in respect of non-consumers) if it satisfies the test of reasonableness under UCTA 1977 and (in respect of consumers) if it is fair under CRA 2015.

CONSUMER PROTECTION ACT 1987

The Consumer Protection Act 1987 (CPA 1987) provides protection for personal injury and some damage to property caused by a defect in a product. Under the Act, if a product is defective the manufacturer will be liable. The claimant does not have to prove duty, care and breach (as they would in negligence), only that the defective product has caused injury. This is called **strict liability**. Anyone along the supply chain dealing with the product can also be liable.

Exam warning

The SQE1 Assessment Specification has identified that candidates need to be familiar with the provisions of the CPA 1987. For example an exam question may ask whether protection can be afforded under the CPA 1987.

Key term: strict liability

This is where a manufacturer of the product is liable without proof of fault.

In order to establish liability under the Act the claimant must show that they have suffered damage caused by a defective product. **Table 7.2** illustrates what needs to be proved under the Act to successfully claim for an injury/damage caused by a defective product.

Table 7.2: Elements to be proved under CPA 1987

Elements under CPA 1987	Definitions
Damage	Includes: • claims for death and personal injury (without limit) • claims for property damage must exceed £275 (s 5(4)) • does not include damage to business property (s 5(2)) • damage to the defective product (replacement/repair) is not covered as this is pure economic loss.
Personal injury	Defined as any disease and any other impairment of a person's physical or mental condition (s 45(1)).
Defect	There is a defect if the safety is not such as persons generally are entitled to expect (s 3). This relates to consumer expectations of the safety of the product and includes products comprised in the product. The following is taken into consideration when determining what persons generally are entitled to expect: • the manner in which and the purpose for which the product has been marketed (whole get up, instructions and warnings) • the expected use of product • the time the product was supplied.
Product	Widely defined in s 1(2) as: • any goods • electricity • a product comprised in another product (component and raw material). Goods defined in s 45(1) as: • substances • growing crops • things comprised in land by virtue of being attached to it • ship • aircraft • vehicle.

Elements to be proved under CPA 1987 (continued)

Elements under CPA 1987	Definitions
Who is liable?	Under s 2(2) defendants include: • the producer of the product (eg manufacturer) • anyone putting his name, mark or trademark on the product, holding himself out to be the producer (eg own branders) • anyone importing from a non-member state of the EU into a member state of the EU • suppliers (but only where they are unable to identify those involved in the supply chain – producers, own branders or importers etc).

The concept of a defect as defined by the CPA 1987 is closely linked to the safety of the product. However, dangerous products may not be found to be defective. Sharp kitchen knives are dangerous but they would not be classified as defective because if they were not sharp they would not be fit for the purpose they are required. **Practice example 7.2** provides an example of how the court has dealt with this point.

Practice example 7.2

The claimants are scalded by very hot coffee (served at a temperature of between 85 and 95°C) at the defendant's fast-food restaurants and bring claims under the CPA 1987. Is the coffee a defective product for the purposes of the Act?

This is what the court had to consider in *Bogle and others v McDonald's Restaurants Ltd* [2002] EWHC 490 (QB). The claimants maintained that the coffee was defective as the temperature it was served at was too high and that the lids provided with the coffee cups came off too easily. The court considered what persons were 'entitled to expect' and held that people expected coffee to be hot and that the lids needed to come off so that customers could add milk and sugar. The claim failed.

In order to establish liability under the Act the claimant must prove causation and show that 'but for' the defect in the product the damage would not have occurred. The claimant can sue any or all of the defendants as liability is joint and several. Liability for defective products cannot be excluded under the CPA 1987.

Defences

The claimant must bring a claim within three years of the injury or damage. The limitation period under the Act is ten years from the date when the product was circulated by the defendant. Defences are dealt with in Section 4 of the Act. **Table 7.3** details the defences available under the CPA 1987.

Table 7.3: Defences under CPA 1987

Section	Defence applicable
4(1)a	Defect is attributable to compliance with legal requirements
4(1)b	Defendant did not supply the product (eg stolen goods)
4(1)c	Defendant did not supply the product in course of business
4(1)d	Defect did not exist in product at time of supply (eg misuse of the product, best before dates on goods)
4(1)e	State of scientific knowledge such that defect was not known and unforeseeable at date of circulation
4(1)f	Manufacturer of component parts is not liable if the finished product is defective and the defect is due to the design of the finished product in line with instructions by the manufacturer of the finished product.

Revision tip

When revising for SQE1 questions on defective products remember that a claim can be brought under both common law and CPA 1987. To satisfy the common law a claimant will need to prove negligence but under CPA 1987 strict liability applies (fault without proof).

Exam warning

When considering SQE1 questions on defective products remember that if the defendant is found liable under the common law (negligence) the defendant will need to cover the cost of the defective product. If the defendant is found liable under the CPA 1987 the defendant does not have to cover the cost of the defective product; also, the claimant can only recover damages to property as long as it exceeds £275 in value.

■ KEY POINT CHECKLIST

This chapter has covered the following key knowledge points. You can use these to structure your revision around, making sure to recall the key details for each point, as covered in this chapter.

* Liability for defective products can arise under both common law and statutory law.
* The elements required in establishing whether the defendant is liable for defective products under the common law were established in the narrow rule from *Donoghue*.
* The narrow rule states that a manufacturer of products owes a duty of care to consumers to ensure that the product reaches the consumer in the form in which they left the manufacturer and in the absence of reasonable care, which results in injury or damage to property, the manufacturer will be liable.
* Under common law a manufacturer is anyone who creates the danger which is inherent in the product.
* Under common law products are anything manufactured which is capable of causing injury or damage.
* Under common law the consumer is anyone who may foreseeably be affected by the defective product.
* Under common law the chain of causation may be broken if an intermediary could reasonably be expected to examine the product (which would have revealed the defect) and then fails to do so.
* The defences available under common law are consent, exclusion of liability and contributory negligence.
* In order to hold the defendant liable for a defective product under CPA 1987 the claimant needs to prove that a defect in the product has caused personal injury or damage to property.
* Strict liability (fault without proof) applies to CPA 1987.
* A defect under CPA 1987 relates to the safety of the product and a defect means that the safety of the product is not such as persons generally are entitled to expect.
* A product is defined widely under CPA 1987 as goods, electricity, a component or raw material.
* Goods are defined under CPA 1987 as substances, growing crops, things compromised in land, any ship, aircraft or vehicle.
* Under CPA 1987 potential defendants include producers of the product, those putting their name to the product and anyone importing into a member state from outside a member state. Producers also include manufacturers of component parts.
* The defences available under the CPA 1987 include defects which are attributable to legal compliance: the defendant did not supply

the product, the defendant did not supply the product in the course of business, the defect did not exist at time of supply, scientific knowledge was such that the defect was unknown at the time and the defect is attributable to the design or compliance with the manufacturer's instructions.

■ KEY TERMS AND CONCEPTS

• strict liability (**page 140**)

■ SQE1-STYLE QUESTIONS

QUESTION 1

The claimant, a purchaser of woollen underpants from the defendant's company, suffers the skin condition dermatitis following wearing the defendant's garments. The claimant did not wash the garments prior to wearing them. It is established that the skin condition has been caused by sulphites left in the defendant's products following the manufacturing process.

Which of the following is likely to be the position of the court when considering whether the defendant is liable at common law for the defective underpants?

A. The court is not likely to find the defendant liable for the claimant's injury as there is no negligence in the manufacturing process.

B. The court will only find the defendant liable if the claimant can prove the manufacturing process was careless.

C. The court is likely to find the defendant liable as presence of sulphites in the garments suggests that at some stage in the manufacturing process the defendant's employees have been careless.

D. The court is not likely to find the defendant liable having done everything expected to ensure the garments are safe.

E. The court is likely to find the defendant liable but reduce the claimant's compensation for failing to wash the garments before wearing them.

QUESTION 2

The claimant injures himself using his employer's chisel. The chisel has been made by the second defendant following the design supplied to them by his employer (first defendant). The chisel is made of alloyed steel which is supplied to the second defendant by a third party. This is the second time the chisel has injured the employee due to a defect in the chisel. The defect in the chisel is due to the manufacturing process used by the third party.

Which of the following is likely to be the position of the court when considering the first defendant's argument that the third party should be liable as the defect is due to the third party's manufacturing process?

A. The court is likely to find the third party liable as they manufactured the chisel and could not have expected either the first or second defendant to examine the tool for defects.
B. The court is likely to find liability attaches to the first defendant as they were aware of the defect in the chisel as it had injured the claimant in a previous incident and they should have withdrawn it from circulation.
C. The court is likely to find both the first and second defendants equally at fault as one designed the faulty product and the other manufactured it.
D. The court is likely to find that liability attaches to the second defendant as they should have inspected the product for defects prior to use.
E. The court is likely to find the claimant at fault on the basis that he knew the chisel was defective but carried on using it.

QUESTION 3

The claimant purchases a hairdryer costing £60 and is in the process of drying his hair when the hairdryer explodes, causing him severe burns to his hand and face. As the hairdryer explodes it falls onto the claimant's bed and sets it alight. The fire spreads to the curtains and the claimant's bedroom suffers extensive damage.

Which of the following is likely to be the court's approach to the claimant's claim brought under the Consumer Protection Act (CPA) 1987?

A. The court is likely to find that a defect in the hairdryer resulted in injury and property damage and will award the claimant damages in respect of personal injury, the cost of the hairdryer and cost of replacing all damaged property.

B. The court is likely to find that a defect in the hairdryer resulted in injury and property damage and will award the claimant damages in respect of personal injury, the cost of the hairdryer and cost of replacing all damaged property as long as the total exceeds £275.

C. The court will hold the defendant liable if the claimant can prove that the defendant manufacturer of the hairdryer has been negligent in the manufacturing process and the court will award damages for personal injury and the cost of replacing all damaged property (including the hairdryer), as long as the total exceeds £275.

D. The court will hold the defendant liable if the claimant can prove that a defect in the product resulted in injury and the court will award damages only for personal injury and the cost of replacing all damaged property (except the hairdryer), as long as the total exceeds £275.

E. The court will only hold the defendant liable if they consider that the hairdryer should have been subject to an intermediate examination by the claimant himself.

QUESTION 4

The claimant contracts Hepatitis C following a blood transfusion from infected donors. The risk of infection is known but there is no process by which the donors' blood can be tested for Hepatitis C and the risk of infection cannot be prevented.

Which of the following is likely to be the court's approach to the claimant's claim brought under the Consumer Protection Act (CPA) 1987?

A. The court will find that blood is not a product as it is not manufactured but exists naturally and the claim will fail under the CPA 1987.

B. The court will find that blood is not a product but that an industrial process is involved in its preparation and if a defect occurs in that process the defendant will be liable if they could have avoided it.

C. The court will find that blood is a product and its preparation an industrial process but will not hold the defendant liable as the state of scientific knowledge at the time was such that the defect could not have been avoided.

D. The court will find that blood is a product and its preparation an industrial process but will not hold the defendant liable as the public's expectation of having uncontaminated blood was unrealistic.

E. The court will find that blood is a product and its preparation an industrial process and will hold the defendant liable as the public has an expectation of having uncontaminated blood products.

QUESTION 5

The claimant is a thief who breaks into an industrial unit where electronic goods are manufactured. The thief steals a number of laptops and sells them to friends. He keeps one laptop for his own personal use. Unknown to the thief the laptops all contain a manufacturing fault. The claimant is injured when plugging in the laptop and suffers severe burns from electrocution. The laptop sets on fire and is destroyed.

Which of the following is likely to be the court's approach to the claimant's claim brought under the Consumer Protection Act (CPA) 1987?

A. The court will find that the manufacturer is liable under the CPA 1987 for the claimant's injuries and damage to the laptop.

B. The court will find that the manufacturer has a complete defence to the claim as the manufacturer did not supply the product to the claimant.

C. The court will find that the manufacturer is liable as persons are generally entitled to expect that laptops are manufactured without defects.

D. The court will find that the manufacturer is liable only in respect of the claimant's personal injury but not for the damage to the laptop.

E. The court will find the manufacturer liable for the claimant's injuries and damage to the laptop but reduce the claimant's damages on the basis the claimant stole the laptop.

■ ANSWERS TO QUESTIONS

Answers to 'What do you know already?' questions at the start of the chapter

1) The common law duty is defined in *Donoghue v Stevenson* [1932] AC 562 (HL). The claimant must prove that the defendant was the

manufacturer, that the (dangerous) item was a product and that the claimant was a consumer, and further, that the product reached the claimant in the form it left the manufacturer.

2) The defences available under common law are consent, contributory negligence and where the manufacturer has excluded liability.

3) They are all considered to be manufacturers, as is anyone who has created a danger which is inherent in the product.

4) True – where any damage is caused wholly or partly by a defect in a product, liability attaches for the damage.

5) No, under Section 7, it is not possible to exclude liability under CPA 1987.

Answers to end-of-chapter SQE1-style questions

Question 1:

The correct answer was C. This is because the court is likely to find the defendant liable as there is unlikely to be any other explanation as to the presence of sulphites in the garments other than the fact that one of the defendant's employees has been careless. This suggests the defendant has been negligent as you would not expect underpants to give you a skin condition. Nor is it reasonable to expect that garments should be washed before use.

A is wrong because there is no other explanation other than negligence in the manufacturing process for the presence of sulphites in the garments.

B is wrong because the manufacturer has not taken reasonable care in making the garments if sulphites are present in the underpants.

D is wrong because the defendant has failed to do everything expected if sulphites are present in the underpants.

E is wrong because it is not reasonable to wash garments before use and there is no reference to an instruction to the consumer to do so.

Question 2:

The correct answer was B. This is because the court is likely to find liability attaches to the first defendant as they were aware of the defect in the chisel as it had injured the claimant in a previous incident and they should have withdrawn it from circulation. This is based on a real case where the court found that the defect occurred in the heat treatment of the alloyed steel by the third party but that there was no probability of the first or second defendant examining the product for defects. The fact the first defendant was aware of the defect due to the previous incident was enough for the court to find them at fault.

A is wrong because the third party manufactured the chisel based on the design of the first defendant.

C is wrong because although the defect occurred in the heat treatment of the steel there was no probability of the first or second defendant examining the steel for defects.

D is wrong because there was no probability of the second defendant examining the product.

E is wrong because the claimant has no choice but to use the product provided by his employer.

Question 3:

The correct answer was D. This is because the court will hold the defendant liable if the claimant can prove that a defect in the product resulted in injury and the court will award damages only for personal injury and the cost of replacing all damaged property (except the hairdryer), as long as the total exceeds £275. Under CPA 1987 all the claimant needs to do is prove that the defect in the hairdryer caused the injury. The court will award damages for loss of or any damage to the claimant's personal property and it must exceed £275. Once property damage exceeds £275 the claimant will receive the full amount. The court will also award damages for personal injury. The claimant will not receive the cost of the hairdryer as this is pure economic loss.

A and B are wrong because under the CPA 1987 the claimant cannot recover the cost of replacing or repairing the hairdryer.

C is wrong because the court will hold the defendant liable if the claimant can prove that a defect in the product resulted in injury (not that the defendant has been negligent in the manufacturing process) as strict liability applies.

E is wrong because the CPA 1987 does not require consumers to carry out examinations of products for defects.

Question 4:

The correct answer was E. This is because the court will find that blood is a product and its preparation an industrial process and will hold the defendant liable as the public has an expectation of having uncontaminated blood products. This is based on a real case where the court accepted that blood was a product and its preparation was an industrial process. The defendant tried to defend the claim on the basis of s 4(1)e, namely, that the state of scientific knowledge was such that they were unable to test for Hepatitis C in the blood of donors and thus they were unable to detect it. The duty on a defendant under CPA 1987 is an onerous one.

A is wrong because blood is a product due to the fact it undergoes an industrial process in order to be prepared for use.

B is wrong because blood is a product for the purposes of CPA 1987.

C is wrong because the duty under the CPA 1987 is onerous on defendants and, irrespective of the state of scientific knowledge, the public have an expectation of receiving uncontaminated blood.

D is wrong because the public have an expectation of receiving blood free from viruses.

Question 5:

The correct answer was B. This is because under s 4(1)b of the CPA 1987 the manufacturer would not be liable as they did not supply the product, the claimant stole it.

A and D are wrong because there is no liability under the CPA 1987 for stolen products.

C is wrong because although persons are generally entitled to expect laptops to be safe, the laptop was stolen and the manufacturer has a complete defence to the claim.

E is wrong because contributory negligence only applies when the defendant has been found liable but the claimant has contributed to his injuries.

■ KEY CASES, RULES, STATUTES AND INSTRUMENTS

The SQE1 Assessment Specification has identified that candidates are required to be familiar with the following:

• Consumer Protection Act 1987

8

Nuisance and *Rylands v Fletcher*

■ MAKE SURE YOU KNOW

This chapter concentrates on the tort of public and private nuisance which aims to protect individuals' proprietary rights. It will also cover the rule in *Rylands v Fletcher*. You are required to know the principles in public and private nuisance and the rule in *Rylands v Fletcher*, and apply the legal principles and rules appropriately and effectively to realistic client-based ethical problems and situations for your SQE1 assessment.

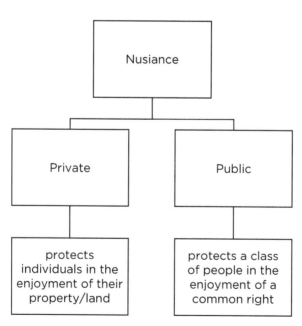

Private and public nuisance

■ SQE ASSESSMENT ADVICE

As you work through this chapter, remember to pay particular attention in your revision to:
• when a claim in private nuisance can be brought
• when a claim in public nuisance can be brought
• when liability under the rule in *Rylands v Fletcher* arises
• remedies and defences for both public and private nuisance and for claims brought under the rule in *Rylands v Fletcher*.

■ WHAT DO YOU KNOW ALREADY?

Have a go at these questions before reading this chapter. If you find some difficult or cannot remember the answers, make a note to look more closely at that during your revision.

1) What are the essential elements required in proving a claim in private nuisance?
   [Private nuisance, pages 154–158]
2) What defences are effective to a claim in private nuisance?
   [Private nuisance, pages 154–158]
3) The two requirements that need to be satisfied in order to succeed in a claim for public nuisance are the nuisance must have affected _____ and the claimant has suffered _____
   [Public nuisance, pages 158–160]
4) True or false?
   It is a defence to a claim in public nuisance that the activity has been continuing for a long period of time.
   [Public nuisance, pages 160–164]
5) What are the defences available under the rule in *Rylands v Fletcher*?
   [Rule in *Rylands v Fletcher*, page 169]

NUISANCE

Nuisance is the tort which deals with interference with land. At common law there are two types of nuisance: private and public. We will first consider private and public nuisance and then the rule in *Rylands v Fletcher*, which deals with a special category of private nuisance.

PRIVATE NUISANCE

Private nuisance is concerned with the unreasonable interference with land (including property) and recognises the fact that a person should be free to enjoy their property and land. **Figure 8.1** highlights some examples of private nuisance.

Key term: private nuisance

Private nuisance is an unlawful interference with a person's use or enjoyment of land. For example, tree roots causing damage to a neighbour's property.

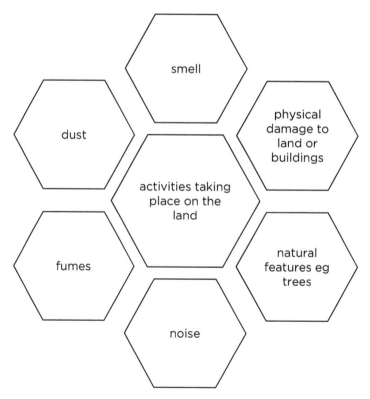

Figure 8.1: Examples of private nuisance

In order to bring a claim in private nuisance there are certain requirements. **Table 8.1** considers who can claim and who can be sued.

Table 8.1: Who can claim and who can be sued?

Who can sue?	Who can be sued?
Only those with exclusive possession rights to the land or property, ie, owner or occupier (tenant if in occupation). For example, guests at a hotel disturbed by loud music from bars close by are unable to pursue a claim in private nuisance as they are only guests and only occupy the hotel room, they have no right to exclusive possession of the room.	• the creator of the nuisance • the occupier of the land • a landlord that authorises a nuisance.

In order to successfully bring a claim in private nuisance there must be interference with the claimant's use and enjoyment of the land and that interference must be unlawful. There are three different types of unlawful interference. These are:
• encroachment onto a neighbour's land
• direct physical injury to a neighbour's land
• interference with enjoyment of land.

Unreasonable/unlawful interference
The use of the land must be unreasonable in order to successfully claim private nuisance. If interference with the claimant's enjoyment of their land is a foreseeable consequence of the defendant's use of their land, that interference will be unreasonable and the defendant will be liable. **Table 8.2** details the factors the court takes into consideration when deciding whether the use of land is unreasonable.

Table 8.2: Unreasonable use of land: relevant factors

Factor taken into consideration	When is this factor relevant?	Example case
Duration/ frequency of the nuisance	Always taken into consideration	Duration and frequency are important. The nuisance must be continuous. The longer the nuisance has lasted the more likely the court will find it unreasonable. In *De Keysers Royal Hotel Ltd v Spicer Bros* (1914) 30 TLR 257 pile driving at night (to build foundations for a new building), even though a temporary operation, was sufficient for the court to find the interference unreasonable and constituting a private nuisance.

Unreasonable use of land: relevant factors (continued)

Factor taken into consideration	When is this factor relevant?	Example case
Character of the neighbourhood	Sometimes (depends upon type of claim)	If the activity being carried out is not in keeping with the area the court will find it unreasonable. In *Hirose Electrical UK Ltd v Peak Ingredients Ltd* [2011] EWCA Civ 987 the court found that the strong smell of food additives from the defendant's premises were not an actionable nuisance as the premises were situated on a light industrial unit and the claimant (an electrical manufacturer) had to tolerate the odours due to the nature of the area.
Sensitivity of the claimant	Sometimes (if relevant to claim)	Reasonable use of land does not become unreasonable due to the fact that it affects a sensitive user of the land/property. In *Robinson v Kilvert* (1889) 41 Ch D 88(CA) the heat from the defendant's manufacturing process damaged the claimant's (heat-sensitive) paper stored on the ground floor of the same building. The court held that the damage was due to the sensitivity of the claimant's paper not the defendant's trade.
Public benefit	Rarely considered	The court may allow an activity that constitutes a private nuisance to continue if the public interest in the continuation outweighs the claimant's right to have the activity stopped. In *Hatton v UK* [2003] 37 EHRR 611 the court referenced the fact that allowing night flights (which disturbed local residents near Heathrow airport) was beneficial to the country's economy.

Unreasonable use of land: relevant factors (continued)

Factor taken into consideration	When is this factor relevant?	Example case
Malice of the defendant	Sometimes (if relevant to the claim)	If the court find that the defendant is committing a nuisance due to unreasonable malice or ill will the court is likely to find the interference unreasonable. In *Christie v Davey* (1893) 1 Ch 316 the claimant was a music teacher and her family also enjoyed playing musical instruments. The defendant neighbour took to making noise (shouting, banging trays) whenever the claimant played music. The court found the defendant liable in private nuisance due to the fact he had acted only to annoy the claimant.

Exam warning

When considering SQE questions about private nuisance remember that it is only actionable if the claimant suffered injury, harm or damage. If the claimant's property or land suffered physical damage the court will find that the interference is unreasonable and the claim will succeed.

Practice example 8.1 illustrates how the court considers the elements of private nuisance.

Practice example 8.1

Residents of an area of London that underwent property development experienced interference with their television signals due to the developers building a 235m tower block in the area. The claimants were occupants of homes in the area and included family relatives, lodgers and other residents that did not have exclusive possession of the properties affected. Do the claimants without a proprietary interest have the right to claim for private nuisance and is interference with television signals interference with the enjoyment of land?

This is what the court had to decide in *Hunter v Canary Wharf* [1997] AC 655 (HL). The court considered that only those with

a proprietary interest were entitled to bring a claim in private nuisance. Children, lodgers and others without a proprietary interest were unable to bring a claim. (The court recognised that a wife with beneficial interest in the family home would have a proprietary interest in the property.) Further, that in order to succeed the interference had to emanate from the defendant's land. As the defendant's building only got in the way of the television signal it fell short of emanating from the land. The claim failed.

PUBLIC NUISANCE

Public nuisance is a tort and also a crime and involves personal injury or harm suffered by the community or a section of the community. In order to successfully claim, the nuisance must affect:
• a class of people and
• the claimant must have suffered special damage.

The difference between public and private nuisance relates to 'who' is affected by the nuisance. In private nuisance it will be those with exclusive proprietary interests (eg, owners, tenants), whereas with public nuisance it will be a group/class of citizens (eg, local residents). Most claims are brought on behalf of this class of people by the Attorney General (A-G).

Key term: public nuisance

Public nuisance is an act or omission that materially affects the reasonable comfort and convenience of life of a group or class of people.

Class of people

The court has not defined the number of people who must be affected by the nuisance but will look at the facts of each case and decide whether the nuisance has affected a cross-section of the public. **Table 8.3** highlights who the courts have previously classified within this group.

Table 8.3: Class of people: public nuisance

Class of people	Court held those affected as a class of people
Local community	Locals affected by quarry blasting. *Attorney-General v PYA Quarries [1957] 2 QB 169 (CA)*

Class of people: public nuisance (continued)

Class of people	Court held those affected as a class of people
Groups with common characteristics	Babies suffering birth defects due to dispersal of toxic chemicals from a landfill site. *Corby Group Litigation v Corby District Council* [2009] EWHC 1944 (TCC)
Highway users	Highway users in the vicinity of a golf club's 13th hole from which golf balls often strayed, hitting road users. *Castle v St Augustine's Links* (1922) 38 TLR 615 (DC)
Wider impact on public	Emergency services diverted from the public to answer the defendant's many hoax calls. *Lowrie* [2005] 1 Cr App R (S) 95 (CA)

The courts have refused to find certain individuals qualify as a group or class of people. **Practice example 8.2** illustrates an example of this.

Practice example 8.2

The defendant posted 538 racially offensive and obscene letters to people throughout the country. Did the 538 individuals qualify as a group or class or people?

This is what the court had to consider in *R v Rimmington* [2005] UKHL 63. The court found that the defendant's conduct was aimed at many individuals, not a community or group, and the claim in public nuisance failed.

Special damage

A claim in tort for public nuisance will only succeed if the inconvenience or interference suffered by that class of people is over and above the inconvenience caused to the class. **Practice example 8.3** illustrates this point.

Practice example 8.3

The claimant was hit by a golf ball and injured. The golf balls leaving the golf course and landing on the high street were a regular occurrence and this affected a section of highway users. Was the claimant able to claim in public nuisance?

> This is what the court had to consider in *Castle v St Augustine's Links* (1922) 38 TLR 615 (DC). Because the claimant had been affected over and above other highway users as he was injured by the golf ball he was able to successfully claim in public nuisance.

Table 8.4 explains who can claim and who can be sued.

The following type of damage can be claimed for:
• damage to property
• personal injury
• economic loss.

Table 8.4: Who can claim and who can be sued?

Who can sue?	Who can be sued?
• Anyone affected by the public nuisance can sue – they do not need to have an interest in the land. In *Corby* (see **Table 8.3**) the affected children had no interest in the land where the nuisance originated from. • The Attorney-General Public nuisance is a crime and the A-G will bring the action on behalf of the affected class of people. • Local authority A local authority has statutory power to bring a claim on behalf of its residents. • An individual In tort the damage suffered by the individual must be over and above that suffered by the class.	• the creator of the nuisance • the person responsible for the nuisance.

DEFENCES

The following defences applicable to private and public nuisance have been covered in **Chapter 4**:
• consent (voluntary acceptance of the nuisance)
• contributory negligence.

Table 8.5 covers the additional defences which are specific to both private and public nuisance. However, the defence of prescription is only available to private nuisance.

Table 8.5: Defences to private and public nuisance

Defences	Example	Effectiveness of defence
Prescription: (Only available to private nuisance.) If the unreasonable user of the land has been using the land in an unreasonable manner for more than 20 years the claim will fail. Time runs from when the claimant became aware of the activity.	In *Sturges v Bridgman* [1879] LR 11 Ch D 852 (CA) the defence of prescription failed as time runs from when the claimant became aware of the activity. A doctor's consulting rooms were disturbed by the noise from the defendant's confectionary business. Although the confectioner had worked at his premises for more than 20 years, the activity only became a nuisance when the doctor extended his premises and his examination rooms were situated closer to the confectioner's premises.	Likely to succeed: Had the doctor in *Sturges* put up with the noise for 20 years and then sought to claim, the defendant could have defended the claim on the basis of 20 years prescription.
Statutory authority: If the activity has been authorised by legislation the claim will fail.	In *Allen v Gulf Oil Refining Ltd* [1981] AC 1001 (HL) an oil company wanted to extend their oil refinery in Wales and the claimant claimed against them in public nuisance. However, the extension was expressly permitted by the Gulf Oil Refinement Act 1965 and the oil company successfully defended the claim as they had statutory authority for their actions.	Likely to succeed
Act of God: If the nuisance is due to an act of nature or an 'act of God' the claim may fail. If the defendant knows about the nuisance and allows it to continue or has had a hand in creating the nuisance the claim may succeed.	In *Greenock Corporation v Caledonian Railway* [1917] AC 556 (HL) the defendants constructed a children's paddling pool which caused the claimant's railway to flood when there was unprecedented heavy rainfall. The defendant's argued that the flooding was due to an act of God (heavy rainfall). The court disagreed and found that the construction of the paddling pool had obstructed the natural flow of the water and the defendant was liable.	Likely to succeed: Had the defendants in *Greenock* not constructed a paddling pool and the heavy rainfall had flooded the railway this would be viewed as an 'act of God'.

Defences to private and public nuisance (continued)

Defences	Example	Effectiveness of defence
Unforeseeable act of a stranger: If the nuisance is due to the act of a stranger or trespasser the claim will fail.	In *Barker v Herbert* [1911] 2 KB 633 (CA) the defendant owned vacant land but had erected railings around the land to prevent people accessing it. Unbeknown to the defendant, children removed some of the railings which allowed the claimant to gain access. The claimant was injured on the land. The defendants were held not liable as they had inspected the premises a few days prior to the incident and the railings were intact.	Likely to succeed
Necessity: If the defendant's actions are reasonable and there is an imminent threat to life or limb (possibly property) the claim will fail.	In *Southport Corporation v Esso Petroleum* [1956] AC 218 (HL) the defendants (oil tanker owners) discharged oil into an estuary in an attempt to prevent the oil tanker breaking up, which would have put the lives of those onboard in danger. The defendants were not liable in private nuisance for the oil spill due to the imminent threat to life.	Likely to succeed
Planning permission: The granting of planning permission does not make the activity lawful (local authority decisions cannot prevent the right to claim nuisance).	In *Wheeler v JJ Saunders* [1996] Ch 19 (CA) the defendant had been granted planning permission to build pig units on his land. The court found that the smell and noise constituted a nuisance irrespective of any planning permission the defendant had been granted.	Unlikely to succeed

Defences to private and public nuisance (continued)

Defences	Example	Effectiveness of defence
Claimant came to the nuisance: The court is unlikely to accept as a defence that a claimant has moved to the area where the activity is taking place.	In *Coventry v Lawrence* [2014] UKSC 13 the claimants had operated a race track where car racing in some form had taken place for over 30 years (causing noise and fumes). The defendant's argument that the claimants had moved to the nuisance years after the race track had been established was rejected by the court.	Unlikely to succeed
Public benefit: If the nuisance is a by-product of an activity which benefits the community the court may be reluctant to grant an injunction stopping the activity but may instead offer an alternative remedy of damages.	In *Coventry v Lawrence* [2014] UKSC 13 the court found that the noise and fumes from the defendant's race track was a nuisance but considered the public benefit of its existence (visitors boosting economy, locals having employment) and did not order the activity to stop (injunction) but awarded the claimant compensation (damages).	Unlikely to succeed but may be reflected in remedy ordered by the court
Contributors to nuisance: It is no defence to a claim that had the defendant's activity occurred in isolation it would not amount to a nuisance.	For example, in a residential town centre area with a street of many nightclubs an argument from one nightclub owner that loud music emitting from their nightclub is not a nuisance if it was considered in isolation without the effect of the other many clubs would fail. The court would not accept that the nuisance only occurs because of the other many nightclubs playing loud music too.	Unlikely to succeed

Revision tip

It is important to understand that some defences will fail, but you need to be aware of those that will not succeed in order to fully consider any SQE1 questions on nuisance and defences.

REMEDIES

The two main remedies consist of either an injunction to prevent the activity or damages to compensate the claimant affected by the nuisance.

Injunctions

An injunction is a court order which prevents the activity causing the nuisance to continue. Failing to comply with an injunction is contempt of court which could lead to a fine or imprisonment for the defendant. **Table 8.6** details the different injunctions available.

Table 8.6: Injunctions

Type of injunction	Description
Prohibitory	Prevents the defendant from doing the activity causing the nuisance and is the most common remedy.
Mandatory	Compels the defendant to rectify the situation that has been caused by the nuisance. These injunctions are used only in certain circumstances.
Quia timet	Obtained before the activity amounting to a nuisance can take place (eg music festival). Only granted where: • high likelihood the nuisance will occur • the activity would cause damage and disruption to the claimant • the defendant will not stop their intended course of action without an injunction.
Interim/final	An interim injunction is a temporary measure which prevents the defendant from continuing with the activity causing the nuisance until such time as the court can consider the matter fully and if appropriate order a final injunction.

As the remedy for nuisance seeks to balance the rights of the parties, which may require a compromise between users of neighbouring land, the court may award an injunction limiting the activity causing the nuisance. **Practice example 8.4** illustrates how the courts deal with this point.

Practice example 8.4

The defendants run a water sports company close to the claimant's property. The claimant built a house at the side of the lake and complains when the noise and frequency of the motorboat racing events increase on the basis they are interfering with her enjoyment of her land. The court accepts that the noise is a private nuisance. Should the court grant an injunction which would prevent all water sports from taking place or should the court order damages to the claimant to compensate her for the nuisance?

This was the issue the court had to consider in the case of *Kennaway v Thompson* [1981] QB 88 (CA). The court ordered an injunction, which did not prohibit the activity in its entirety but limited the defendant club's racing activities in each year and restricted the noise levels of the motorboats. In doing so the court balanced the rights of the claimant with the rights of the defendant. An injunction preventing all motorboat activity would have made the water sports centre unworkable.

Revision tip

Injunctions are an equitable remedy and in order for the court to grant one the claimant must have acted promptly, not encouraged or agreed to the nuisance and the defendant must be able to comply with the injunction.

Exam warning

When considering SQE1 questions on remedies available for private and public nuisance, remember that a claimant will only be awarded an injunction where damages would not be deemed to be an appropriate remedy.

Damages

Damages (monetary compensation) can be awarded by the court for any losses suffered by the claimant up until the date of trial. The court does have limited powers to order damages for future losses. The court will award damages for physical damage to land (eg, damage to a building exterior due to emittance of smoke/chemicals) and also in relation to personal discomfort/inconvenience (eg, being unable to use your garden due to the smell/dust).

In considering which remedy to award, the court will take into consideration whether the claimant has made out the case for the granting of an injunction. If the court decides not to grant an injunction they will award damages. The court can exercise its discretion and is likely to refuse an injunction and award damages where the harm suffered by the claimant is:
• small, and
• can be quantified in financial terms, and
• can be compensated by damages, and
• it would be oppressive to grant an injunction.

The court is more likely to award damages where compensation would remedy the situation. Not all of the four tests above need to be satisfied. The court will also consider whether the granting of an injunction would affect the public interest. An example of this would be where the defendant is an employer of many employees and an injunction would effectively mean the business has to close.

Abatement
Abatement relates to the claimant rectifying the nuisance by removing or stopping the nuisance taking place. An example of this may be a claimant whose garden is being encroached upon by a neighbour's tree roots or branches. The claimant would be able to trim the branches/tree roots as long as doing so reasonably. Anything undertaken which is unreasonable could be viewed as trespass.

THE RULE IN *RYLANDS V FLETCHER*
We have considered private and public nuisance. The rule in *Rylands v Fletcher* is another specialised form of private nuisance. It concerns a situation where an escape of non-natural things from a person's land causes damage to property owned by somebody else. The occupier of the land from which the non-natural thing escaped will be liable for the damage, irrespective of whether or not they were actually at fault. In order to understand how the rule operates fully, it is sensible to familiarise yourself with the facts of the case.

Rylands v Fletcher [1868] LR 3 HL 330 (HL) involved a claim brought against defendant mill owners who had engaged experienced and competent independent contractors to build a reservoir to supply water to their mill. The contractors built the reservoir over old mine shafts. Due to the weight of the water the mine shafts collapsed and flooded the claimant's colliery. The claimant could not succeed in private nuisance as the defendant had not been negligent on the basis they had instructed competent contractors. The court found the defendants liable on the basis that *they had brought and collected something 'non-natural' onto their land which foreseeably had caused damage once it escaped.* **Figure 8.2** illustrates how the rule is applied by the court. **Table 8.7** explains the criteria you would need to apply to an SQE1 question to establish whether a party will be liable under the rule in *Rylands v Fletcher.*

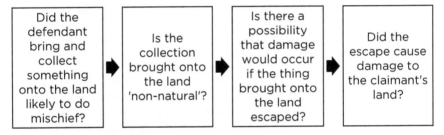

Figure 8.2: The rule in Rylands v Fletcher

Exam warning

The SQE1 Assessment Specification requires candidates to be familiar with the rule in *Rylands v Fletcher*. An exam question may require you to consider whether a claim can be brought under the rule in *Rylands v Fletcher.*

Table 8.7: Elements of the rule in Rylands v Fletcher

Element	Example
Did the defendant bring and collect something onto the land likely to do mischief?	The defendant must bring and collect something on their land which is likely to do a mischief. The court have considered fumes, vapours, cattle and sewerage to fall into this category.

Elements of the rule in Rylands v Fletcher (continued)

Element	Example
Is the collection brought onto the land 'non-natural'?	The rule will not apply to things that are naturally on the land (eg trees, plants). The court takes into consideration the normal use of the land according to the standards of the day. In *Transco plc v Stockport MBC* [2004] 2 AC 1 (HL) the defendant's pipe leaked, causing an embankment to collapse. The collapse affected the claimant's gas pipe which required remedial work. The court found that the use of pipes to supply water was a normal use of the land and the claimant's claim failed.
Is there a possibility that damage would occur if the thing brought onto the land escaped?	The thing collected on the land must be likely to do mischief if it escapes. The thing must also move from land occupied/controlled by the defendant to land not occupied/controlled by the defendant. In *Stannard (t/a Wyern Tyres) v Gore* [2012] EWCA Civ 1248 the defendants stored tyres on their land which caught fire. The fire spread to the claimant's premises. The claim failed as the court found that the 'thing' brought onto the land were the tyres (which were not a mischief if they escaped) and not the fire which started or increased the thing.
Did the escape cause damage to the claimant's land?	The thing collected on the land does not in itself have to be dangerous, but it must be reasonably foreseeable to cause damage if it escapes. This principle was introduced by *Cambridge Water Co Ltd v Eastern Counties Leather plc* [1994] 2 AC 264 (HL). The defendant's use of solvents in their tanning process for over 20 years had polluted the water used by the claimants, causing the claimant to incur the cost of relocating the source of their water (well). The claim failed as the court held that it was not foreseeable that the chemicals would seep through the land and pollute the water extracted by the claimants.

The rule in *Rylands v Fletcher* is concerned with rights and duties in respect of an occupier's land. An essential element of the tort is that there is an escape from the defendant's land. **Practice example 8.5** illustrates how the court has dealt with this issue.

Practice example 8.5

The claimant is working for the Ministry of Supply during the Second World War and is required to inspect a munitions factory when a shell explodes and she is injured. There is no negligence on the part of her employer. Is she able to claim under the rule in *Rylands v Fletcher* for the escape of the hazardous material?

This is what the court had to consider in *Read v J Lyons* [1947] AC 156 (HL). The court found that a shell exploding did not qualify as an escape of anything dangerous from the defendant's premises to the claimant's premises.

Defences

The following defences applicable to claims brought under the rule in *Rylands v Fletcher* have been covered in **Chapter 4 Defences**:
• consent (voluntary acceptance of the nuisance)
• contributory negligence.

The following defences also applicable to claims brought using the rule in *Rylands v Fletcher* have been covered earlier in the chapter:
• statutory authority
• act of God
• unforeseeable act of a stranger.

Remedies

If a claim succeeds under the rule in *Rylands v Fletcher* the claimant will receive damages. A claimant cannot bring a claim for personal injury.

■ KEY POINT CHECKLIST

This chapter has covered the following key knowledge points. You can use these to structure your revision around, making sure to recall the key details for each point, as covered in this chapter.
• Nuisance seeks to protect peoples' rights and enjoyment of their land. Private nuisance protects land and property from unreasonable interference and public nuisance seeks to protect the comfort and convenience of the public.

- In order to bring a claim in private nuisance the claimant must have the right to exclusive possession of the property/land affected, the use of the property/land must be unreasonable and the claimant must have suffered some harm, injury or damage.
- Interference with property/land which results in physical damage to the claimant's property/land will always be unreasonable.
- When considering whether interference is unreasonable the court may take into consideration the character of the locality, duration of the interference, sensitivity of the claimant, any public benefit and any malice on the part of the defendant.
- In order to bring a claim in public nuisance the claimant must belong to a class/group of people and the claimant must suffer damage over and above the inconvenience caused to the group.
- General defences of consent and contributory negligence are available for private and public nuisance.
- Effective defences available to private nuisance are prescription, statutory authority, act of God, unforeseeable act of a stranger and necessity.
- Effective defences available to public nuisance are statutory authority, act of God, unforeseeable act of a stranger and necessity.
- Coming to the nuisance, public benefit and acts in isolation are unlikely to succeed as defences to either private or public nuisance.
- Remedies for private and public nuisance include damages and/or an injunction.
- There are different types of injunctions available to the court (prohibitory, mandatory, quia timet, interim or final).
- The rule in *Rylands v Fletcher* relates to a type of private nuisance with specialised rules.
- In order to be liable under the rule in *Rylands v Fletcher* the defendant must have collected and kept something non-natural on their land which is likely to do mischief if it escapes.
- The claimant must have suffered harm/property damage, but cannot claim personal injury under the rule in *Rylands v Fletcher*.
- The defences applicable to a claim brought under the rule in *Rylands v Fletcher* are contributory negligence, consent, statutory authority, act of God and unforeseeable act of a stranger.
- The claimant will be awarded damages if successful under the rule in *Rylands v Fletcher*.

■ KEY TERMS AND CONCEPTS

- private nuisance (**page 154**)
- public nuisance (**page 158**)

■ SQE1-STYLE QUESTIONS

QUESTION 1

The claimant owns a property backing onto the railway line. The railway company are aware of the plant 'Japanese knotweed' (known to damage buildings if left untreated) which is growing close to the line and encroaching on the claimant's property.

Which of the following is likely to be the position of the court when considering whether the defendant is liable in private nuisance for the encroachment of Japanese knotweed on the claimant's property?

A. The court is likely to find the defendant not liable in private nuisance as the character of the railway line and surrounding area is rural and the claimant should expect plants to grow around his property.
B. The court will only find the defendant liable if the claimant can prove that the nuisance affects the comfort and convenience of life of a class of people.
C. The court is likely to find the defendant not liable in expecting the railway company to remove the plant as the claimant is being too sensitive to the growing of plants in the vicinity of his property.
D. The court is likely to find the defendant liable as Japanese knotweed is a natural hazard which affects the claimant's ability to use and enjoy the land.
E. The court is likely to find the defendant not liable as the railway line is operated for the benefit of the citizens and the community.

QUESTION 2

The claimant owns a large country estate in an industrial area where many manufacturing companies operate. The claimant lives less than 2 miles from the defendant's smelting works. The vapours from the defendant's smelting processes damage the claimant's trees.

Which of the following is likely to be the position of the court when considering the claim brought in private nuisance by the claimant against the defendant?

A. The court is likely to find the defendant not liable as the claimant lives in an industrial locality.

B. The court is likely to find liability attaches to the defendant as there has been damage to property.

C. The court is likely to find the defendant is not liable as it is likely the nature of the locality has changed over the years from rural to industrial as manufacturing companies came to the area.

D. The court is likely to find that liability attaches to the defendant only if the claimant's enjoyment of the land is adversely affected.

E. The court is likely to find the defendant not liable as the smelting works are for the benefit of the local economy.

QUESTION 3

The claimant organised an 'acid house' party which took place in woods. Starting at 11 P.M. the party continued for 12 hours and thousands of people attended. DJs played loud music, and attendees parked the cars along the roads to the woods. There were no toilets or litter bins in the woods.

Which of the following is likely to be the court's approach as to whether the defendant created a public nuisance?

A. The court is likely to find the claimant committed a public nuisance on the basis that the noise and inconvenience affected locals.

B. The court is unlikely to find the defendant committed a public nuisance as the party only affected some local people.

C. The court will find the duration of the party (12 hours) as insufficient as it was not continuous.

D. The court is unlikely to hold the defendant liable as the party was for the benefit of the public good and enjoyment of the thousands of party goers.

E. The court will accept the defendant's argument that the organisation of the party in isolation did not amount to a nuisance but it was the actions of the party goers which the defendant could not control.

QUESTION 4

A large group of spectators at a football match have their enjoyment of the football match disturbed when the defendant disables the floodlights.

Which of the following is likely to be the court's approach as to whether the defendant created a public nuisance?

A. The court is likely to find the claimant committed a public nuisance on the basis that the convenience and comfort of a class of people have been affected.
B. The court is unlikely to find the defendant committed a public nuisance as the spectators at a football match do not qualify as a class of people.
C. The court will find the spectators have not suffered damage over and above other local residents and the claim will fail.
D. The court is unlikely to hold the defendant liable as the spectators have come to the nuisance by attending the football ground.
E. The court will accept the defendant's argument that the claimants have not suffered damage to property by the disabling of the floodlights.

QUESTION 5

The claimant suffers inconvenience (headaches), including the death of animals raised on his land, due to the escape of gas from the defendant's disused mines close to his property. The gas accumulates in mine shafts and mixes with oxygen to produce gas which when concentrated in air (and lack of wind/ventilation) can cause loss of consciousness and death.

Which of the following is likely to be the court's approach to the claimant's claim brought under the rule in *Rylands v Fletcher*?

A. The court will likely find the defendant liable for the escape of a non-natural substance onto the claimant's land.
B. The court will likely find the defendant not liable as the escape of gas has affected only individuals and not a class of people.
C. The court will likely find the defendant liable due to collecting and keeping the gas in the mine shafts on their land and allowing it to escape.
D. The court will likely find the defendant not liable as mining activity is a natural use of the land and the gas has not been brought onto the land by the defendant.
E. The court will likely find the defendant liable as it was foreseeable that an unused mineshaft would emit toxic gas and do mischief by damaging property once it escaped.

■ ANSWERS TO QUESTIONS

Answers to 'What do you know already?' questions at the start of the chapter

1) The essential elements required in proving a claim in private nuisance are that the claimant has a proprietary interest in the land and the defendant's interference is unreasonable.
2) Effective defences to a claim in private nuisance are prescription, statutory authority, act of God, unforeseeable act of a stranger and necessity.
3) The two requirements that need to be satisfied in order to succeed in a claim for public nuisance are the nuisance must have affected a *class of people* and the claimant has suffered *special damage.*
4) False – Prescription (carrying on an activity which constitutes a nuisance for more than 20 years) is a defence applicable to private nuisance only.
5) The defences available under the rule in *Rylands v Fletcher* are consent, contributory negligence, statutory authority, act of God and unforeseeable act of a stranger.

Answers to end-of-chapter SQE1-style questions

Question 1:
   The correct answer was D. This is because the court is likely to find the defendant liable as Japanese knotweed is a natural hazard which affected the claimant's ability to use and enjoy the land. In order to be actionable in private nuisance there must be unreasonable interference with the land. This is based on a real case where the Japanese knotweed had not yet damaged the claimant's property but the court found that it was such a hazard due to its rapid spread that the claimant could claim loss of amenity (enjoyment) of the land and the cost of treating the soil to prevent the plant spreading.
   A is wrong because irrespective of the rural nature of the area the claimant is entitled to enjoy his land free from Japanese knotweed.
   B is wrong because comfort and convenience of a class of people relates to public nuisance not private nuisance.
   C is wrong because the claimant is not too sensitive. Japanese knotweed grows rapidly and would interfere with the claimant's enjoyment of his land.

E is wrong because the public benefit is not an effective defence to private nuisance.

Question 2:

The correct answer was B. This is because the court is likely to find liability attaches to the defendant as there has been damage to property. This is based on a real case where the defendant tried to argue that the whole locality was industrial and he should be able to continue his smelting activities but the court found that interference will always be unreasonable if it causes damage to property. If the vapours had not caused damage but only personal discomfort the court would take into account the locality and character of the neighbourhood.

A is wrong because interference causing damage to property will always be held to be unreasonable.

C is wrong because locality is not relevant if the nuisance has caused property damage. If the vapours had not caused damage but only personal discomfort the court would take into account the locality and character of the neighbourhood.

D and E are wrong because interference causing damage to property will always be held to be unreasonable.

Question 3:

The correct answer was A. This is because the court is likely to find the claimant committed a public nuisance on the basis that the noise and inconvenience affected locals. This is based on a real criminal case where the defendant's party blocked roads and the party goers dropped litter and left urine and excrement throughout the woods. Locals as far away as 6 miles could hear the noise and vibrations from the sound systems. The public nuisance had affected a class of people and caused discomfort and inconvenience (lack of sleep, blocking roads and the mess left by the party goers).

B is wrong because the local people fall into a class of people.

C is wrong because it is not a requirement of public nuisance (but private nuisance) that the nuisance is continuous.

D is wrong because a party causing noise and disturbance to locals is not for the benefit of the public good.

E is wrong because the defendant committed a public nuisance in organising the party knowing many would attend and there are no isolated activities.

Question 4:

The correct answer was A. This is because the court will find the football spectators are a class of people. This is based on a real case where the defendant was planning to switch the lights off to benefit from gambling on the likelihood of this happening.

B is wrong because spectators in the ground are classed as a group of people.

C is wrong because the spectators do not need to suffer over and above the locals – they just have to qualify as a class of people.

D is wrong because the spectators have attended the match with the intention of watching football, and there is no nuisance until the defendant disables the floodlights.

E is wrong because the spectators have suffered inconvenience which is one of the kinds of damage which fall within the scope of the tort.

Question 5:

The correct answer was D. This is because the court will find the defendant not liable as mining activity is a natural use of the land and the gas has not been brought onto the land by the defendant. This is based on a real case where the claimant's claim failed under the rule in *Rylands v Fletcher* due to the fact that the court found mining and the natural gases emitted did not fall under 'non-natural' use.

A is wrong because mining activity is a natural use of the land.

B is wrong because the escape does not need to affect a class of people under the rule in *Rylands v Fletcher*.

C is wrong because the collection of gas due to mining is a natural use of the land.

E is wrong because mining on the land is a natural use of the land.

■ KEY CASES, RULES, STATUTES AND INSTRUMENTS

The SQE1 Assessment Specification has identified that candidates are required to know the following case:

• *Rylands v Fletcher* [1868] LR 3 HL 330 (HL)

Index

defective products 52-3, 55, 62-3,
136-51; definitions 141-2, 144; safety
contrasts 142, *see also* product
liability
defences 79-95, 113-14, 124-7, 131-6,
139-40, 143-5, 160-4, 169-70;
complete defences 79, 81, 84, 87,
89, 91, 93, 132, 139-40, 144, 148,
151; death claims 60, 82, 125, 140;
definitions 79-89, 139-40, 144,
160-4, 169-70; general defences
80-95, 139-40, 160, 169-70; nuisance
153, 160-4, 169-70; occupier's liability
80, 88, 113-14, 124-7, 131-4; overview
80, 139-40; partial defences 79, 89,
140, 144; private nuisance 153, 158,
160-4, 169-70, 174, 176; product
liability 136, 137, 139-40, 143-5,
149-51; public nuisance 153, 160-4,
170; Rylands v Fletcher rule 169, 170,
174, 176; specific defences 80, 88,
113, *see also* consent; contributory
negligence; illegality
defendants, definition 2-3, *see also*
individual topics
Denning, Lord 86
dentists/patients 3, 20
dependants, death claims 59-61, 71-2,
75, 76
depression 70, 73-4, 77
dermatitis, brick dust 39
diabetic pregnant women 18
distributors 136, 137, *see also* product
liability
doctors/patients 2-3, 7, 13, 16-20, 25,
28-31, 36-8, 44, 49, 59, 70, 86;
damages 59; gross negligence
manslaughter 25; lost chance claims
44, 49, 50-1, 54; pre-treatment

material risks information disclosure
18; professional standard of care
16-18, 20, 28-9, 31, 36, 38, 44, 49-50,
54; special contributory negligence
defence claimants 86; special
standard of care 20, 49-50, 54
Donoghue narrow rule, product liability
135-40, 144, 148-9
drivers *see* road users
drugs' suppliers 88
dust example of nuisance 154, 166
duty of care 1, 3-14, 23-6, 29-32, 36,
63-4, 66-7, 99, 116-24, 137-40;
Caparo three-stage duty of care
test 5-8, 12-13, 14, 26, 29, 30,
31-2, 65; common law 3-7, 8-9, 83,
103-6, 108-12, 135-40, 143-5, 149;
control relationships 3, 6, 9, 11, 13,
67; definition 1, 3-14, 23-6, 29-32,
36, 63-4, 66-7, 99, 116-24, 137-40;
establishing a duty of care 2, 3-4,
5-8, 9, 13, 20, 23, 25-6, 27, 29-32,
63-4, 66, 69, 80, 89, 93, 96-7,
116-24, 137-40, 143-5; flowcharts
3, 7, 14; foresight 2-7, 11-14, 27-32,
45, 57-8, 66-71, 75, 93, 137-40;
incrementally-and-by-analogy duty
of care test 5, 7, 26, 29, 30, 31-2;
neighbour principle 4, 32, 137-40;
occupier's liability 116-27, 131-2;
Occupiers' Liability Act 1957 (OLA
1957) 116-21, 123-7, 131-2; Occupiers'
Liability Act 1984 (OLA 1984) 121-7,
133; omissions special duty of care
8-10; product liability elements
137-40, 144-51; reasonableness 5-8,
12-16, 26, 67, 103-6, 117-24, 132-3,
137-40, 144, 149; special duty of
care problems (omissions and third

Ingram Content Group UK Ltd.
Milton Keynes UK
UKHW031017140523
421698UK00013B/59

9 781914 213069